THE POLITICS
AND ETHICS
OF FIELDWORK

MAURICE PUNCH
The Netherlands School of Business
The Netherlands

Qualitative Research Methods,
Volume 3

SAGE PUBLICATIONS
The International Professional Publishers
Newbury Park   London   New Delhi

For information address:

SAGE Publications, Inc.
2455 Teller Road
Newbury Park, California 91320

SAGE Publications Ltd.
6 Bonhill Street
London EC2A 4PU
United Kingdom

SAGE Publications India Pvt. Ltd.
M-32 Market
Greater Kailash I
New Delhi 110 048 India

International Standard Book Number 0-8039-2562-X
0-8039-2517-4 (pbk.)

Library of Congress Catalog Card No. 85-062291

FOURTH PRINTING, 1991

When citing a University paper, please use the proper form. Remember to cite the correct
Sage University Paper series title and include the paper number. One of the following
formats can be adapted (depending on the style manual used):

(1) AGAR, MICHAEL H. (1985) "Speaking of Ethnography." Sage University Paper
series on Qualitative Research Methods, Volume 2. Beverly Hills, CA: Sage.

OR

(2) Agar, Michael H. 1985. *Speaking of ethnography.* Sage University Paper series on
Qualitative Research Methods (Vol. 2). Beverly Hills, CA: Sage.

CONTENTS

Series Introduction   5

Editors' Introduction   7

Acknowledgments   8

1. Introduction: On the Politics of Fieldwork   11

    Introduction   11
    Coming Clean   14
    The Research Craft   16
    Research Dilemmas   17
    Politics of Research   19
    Factors Influencing Outcomes   21
    Obligations   25
    The Need for Analytical Reflection   26

2. Ethical Considerations in Fieldwork   29

    Introduction   29
    The Issues   31
    Ethical Research Dilemmas   35
    Conclusion   48

3. Dialogue of the Deaf: A Case of Sponsorship and
   "Publicatio Interruptus"   49

    Introduction   49
    Dramatis Personae   51
    Initial Involvement with the Dartington Project 54
    The Fieldwork Period   57
    The Battle over Publication   59
    Conclusions   69

4. Conclusion: Muddy Boots and Grubby Hands   70

    Realities of the Field: Trust, Deceit, and Dissimulation   70
    Research Obligations: Sponsorship, Confidentiality, and the
      Freedom to Publish   74
    Conclusion: Common Sense and Responsibility   80

References   85

About the Authors   93

SERIES INTRODUCTION

Contrast and irony provide the definitional context for this series of monographs on qualitative methods. Contrast is inevitable because the label itself makes sense only when set against something it is not. Irony is also inevitable, as the denotative contrast between the qualitative and quantitative is so often misleading, if not downright false. The mandate for the series is then paradoxical. We wish to highlight the distinctions between methods thought to be qualitative and quantitative, but also to demonstrate that such distinctions typically break down when subjected to scrutiny. Alongside the Sage Series on Quantitative Applications in the Social Sciences comes the Sage Series on Qualitative Research Methods, but the wise reader had best intermingle the monographs of the two sets rather than stack them on separate shelves.

One way of approaching the paradox is to think of qualitative methods as procedures for counting to one. Deciding what is to count as a unit of analysis is fundamentally an interpretative issue requiring judgment and choice. It is, however, a choice that cuts to the core of qualitative methods — where meanings rather than frequencies assume paramount significance. Qualitative work is blatantly interpretative; but, as the work in this series demonstrates, there are a number of increasingly sophisticated procedures to guide the interpretative acts of social researchers.

The monographs in this series go beyond the short confessionals usually found in the methodology sections of research reports. They also go beyond the rather flat, programmatic treatments afforded qualitative methods in most research textbooks. Not only are qualitative methods becoming more variegated, going well beyond the traditional look, listen, and learn dicta issued by traditional field researchers, they are also being shaped more distinctly by explicit philosophical and moral positions. This series seeks to elaborate both qualitative techniques and the intellectual grounds on which they stand.

The series is designed for the novice, eager to learn about specific modes of social inquiry, as well as for the veteran researcher, curious about the widening range of social science methods. Each contribution extends the boundaries of methodological discourse, but not at the expense of losing the uninitiated. The aim is to minimize jargon, make analytic premises visible, provide concrete examples, and limit the scope of each volume with precision and restraint. These are, to be sure, introductory monographs, but each allows for the development of a lively research theme with subtlety, detail, and illustration. To a large extent, each monograph deals with the specific ways qualitative researchers establish norms and justify their craft. We think the time is right to display the rather remarkable growth of qualitative methods in both number and reflective consideration. We are confident that readers of this series will agree.

John Van Maanen
Peter K. Manning
Marc L. Miller

EDITORS' INTRODUCTION

Fieldwork of the sustained, intensive variety necessarily involves the negotiation of trust between the researcher and researched. The limits of trust are tested throughout a study but are perhaps most visible (consequential) at the initiation and publishing phases of social research. Maurice Punch in Volume 3 of the Sage Series on Qualitative Methods takes us backstage in the little dramas of social research where the always provisional character of research agreements are put on display. *The Politics and Ethics of Fieldwork* catalogs and illustrates occasions of trust making and breaking among the many parties who, at various times are actively engaged in and concerned with a research project. This monograph is not, however, a dry *ex cathedra* list of fieldwork do's and don'ts. The writing is vivid, witty, ironic and packed with lively personal detail. There is moral sensitivity here but it is of a most contextual sort. A fieldworker's claim, then, to neutrality, objectivity, descriptive faithfulness, or benign intent is a matter of perspective. That the researched may dispute such claims is the moral of many of Professor Punch's cautionary tales.

John Van Maanen
Peter K. Manning
Marc L. Miller

ACKNOWLEDGMENTS

For help and encouragement in various capacities I would like to express my appreciation to Nic van Dijk, Carl Klockars, Michael Clarke, Nigel Fielding, Al Reiss, Geoffrey Hawthorn, Patricia Williams, Elizabeth Whetton, Spencer Millham, Wim Broer, Peter Manning, Simon Holdaway, Dennis Marsden, Michael Chatterton, and particularly John Van Maanen.

During my research with the Amsterdam Police I noticed that some policemen, but particularly detectives, view the courts as a charade, consider crime reports to be a fiction, and deride criminal statistics as a pack of lies. They are conscious that the art they practice is one of constantly constructing accounts of an ambivalent reality, that their world is one of bending rules, and that they have to manipulate people in order to get information from them. To a certain extent, the fieldworker is no different from the detective. And, while I take the academic enterprise seriously, I must admit that some of the policeman's mocking self-derision at the procedural and ethical acrobatics he is forced to perform rubbed off on me in terms of a skeptical awareness that the situational ethics of fieldwork are almost insuperable. When researchers say that they did not deliberately lie but did not tell the whole truth to the researched, then they make precisely the sort of neutralizing distinction that policemen make when they feel "forced" to lie. Now, when I read reports on fieldwork methods I sniff suspiciously and feel that convention demands that the social scientist appear before the bar of professional standards where peers expect a clinical, sober, black-and-white report of the methodology. Like the policeman in court, the fieldworker can but conform to expectations, endeavoring to keep a straight face and to look honest.

How spouses and families react to the researcher's absence in the field — or, alternatively, constrain his or her presence in the setting — would make an interesting study that might contrast considerably with the obligatory, and often sickening, gratitude to domestic partners displayed in acknowledgments. Americans are particularly obsequious in this respect, although a perusal of their dedications can reveal that the source of affection has changed between publications. I still find it difficult to forgive missing an exciting and dramatic police raid on a Chinese gambling den in Amsterdam because my wife imposed a curfew on my fieldwork, which was backed with chilling sanctions. I am obliged, however, to record my gratitude to Marjon van Tol and Monique van Rooyen at Nijenrode for their nimble typing.

Maurice Punch
Amstelveen, April 1985

You mean they pay you to run with guys like me?
That's a pretty good racket.

Hustler to Polsky (1971, p. 131)

THE POLITICS AND ETHICS OF FIELDWORK
Muddy Boots and Grubby Hands

MAURICE PUNCH
Nijenrode, The Netherlands School of Business

1. INTRODUCTION: ON THE POLITICS OF FIELDWORK

Laughing and joking about buying a bundle of dope, Ralphie turned to the anthropologist and said, "Here's a present for you." The anthropologist felt Ralphie drop a heavy object into his raincoat pocket. It was a loaded snub-nosed revolver .... Urban American fieldwork, then, may confront the researcher with moral, ethical, and legal crises on an almost daily basis. (Soloway and Walters 1977, pp. 172, 176)

Introduction

"Infiltration" constitutes the key skill in field methods. Here I am assuming that qualitative fieldwork employs participant observation as its central technique and that this involves the researcher in prolonged immersion in the life of a group, community, or organization in order to learn about people's habits and thoughts. Clearly, qualitative research covers a number of techniques (but principally observation, interviewing, and documentary analysis), and these are employed in varying degrees in several disciplines, including sociology, anthropology, organizations, criminal justice, social work, medicine, education, industrial relations, and social psychology. While the classical anthropologist normally spent lengthy celibate periods among his "tribe," contemporary researchers are to be found within a bewildering variety of groups and institutions involving differing time-spans and types of involvement, including prisons, communes, sects, mental hospitals, reservations, public rest

11

rooms, welfare agencies, street gangs, the police, the military, fishing villages; they are even to be found skulking in morgues, funeral parlors, and embalming units (one obviously cannot pass on peacefully anymore without being observed by a budding ethnographer).

Faced by the daunting task of exploring a gamut of approaches in diverse fields, I have been guided by my own preferences and background in highlighting particularly observational studies within sociology. With the student in mind, I intend running through the sorts of moral and political issues that occur continually in accounts of sociological, and anthropological, fieldwork. While students may become involved in research in various capacities, and may employ a range of techniques of varying levels of formality, many of them first encounter fieldwork in terms of undergraduate assignments or graduate dissertation work in a solo enterprise, with relatively unstructured observation, close involvement in the field, and deep identification with the researched. For instance, a pioneer of field studies, W.F. Whyte, lived for almost four years in "Cornerville," learned Italian, became almost a son to the Martinis (with Mama waiting up for him to come home at night), and clearly had an enduring influence on some of the people he met (cf. Appendix B to the third edition of *Street Corner Society*, 1981).

Far more so than with other styles of social research, then, this approach means that the investigator engages in a close relationship during a considerable period of time with those he or she observes. This is of vital significance, because the development of that relationship is subtly intertwined with both the outcome of the project and the nature of the data. In fieldwork, and this contrasts starkly with more formal methods, the researcher is his own research instrument (Clarke 1975, p. 96), and his reactions tell us something of crucial importance about the nature of the phenomenon he is studying.

Pivotal to the whole relationship between researcher and researched, for instance, is access and acceptance, which is why I have deliberately employed the word "infiltration" above. For this technique has a negative connotation associated with spying and deception:

the only investigators I can think of who enjoyed privileges when engaged in the business of gathering information for their own professional purposes are policemen and espionage agents, and I doubt very much that any of us would like to operate with the general level of trust and respect that they command. (Kai Ericson in Bulmer 1982: p. 150)

Entry and departure, distrust and confidence, elation and despondency, commitment and betrayal, friendship and desertion are as fundamental here as are academic discussions on the techniques of observation, making field notes, analyzing the data, and writing the report. Furthermore, acute moral and ethical dilemmas may be encountered while a semi-conscious political process of negotiation pervades fieldwork. And both elements, political and ethical, often have to be resolved *situationally*, and even spontaneously, without the chance of armchair reflection. How to cope with a loaded revolver dropped in your lap is something you have to resolve on the spot, however much you may have anticipated it in prior training. As such, the social and political processes inextricably surrounding fieldwork are of crucial interest in scrutinizing the method itself. Those processes form the central focus of this book.

The dynamics and dilemmas associated with this area of fieldwork can be summarized crudely in terms of getting in and getting out, and of one's moral and social conduct in relation to the "political" constraints of the field. Potentially, this covers a vast and complex area, and I have chosen to spotlight three major facets of the "politics and ethics" of fieldwork. Chapter 2 deals with ethical considerations related to research. Chapter 3 examines difficulties in the relationship with sponsors in the light of a battle over publication that I experienced early in my career. And the concluding chapter endeavors to summarize the lessons of these chapters in terms that, hopefully, can be of use in warning students and others about predicaments and pitfalls in the relatively unexplored dimension of the "politics" of field research.

To a greater or lesser extent, "politics" suffuses all sociological research. By "political" I mean everything from the micropolitics of personal relations, the cultures and resources of research units and universities, to the powers and policies of government research departments, and ultimately even the state itself. All of these contexts crucially influence the design, implementation, and outcomes of research.

The perspective espoused in this book, of analyzing the largely hidden political and moral agenda of fieldwork, can be of particular utility to the novitiate for two main reasons. First, it may well be that in our teaching and publications we tend to sell students a smooth, almost idealized, model of the research process as neat, tidy, and unproblematic ("the unchanging researcher makes a unilinear journey through a static setting": Hunt 1984, p. 285). Perhaps we should be more open and honest about the actual pains and perils of conducting research in order to prepare and forewarn other aspiring researchers. And, second, this exercise need not necessarily be narcissistic and self-indulgent because it can perform the important function of alerting the fieldworker to the fact that his or her social and emotional involvement in the research setting constitutes an important source of *data*.

At the same time, I do not wish to open the floodgates for sentimental, emotional, pseudo-honest accounts detailing every nervous tremor and moment of depression or elation (cf. Kirkham 1974). There is a difference between reproducing one's research diary — which fieldworkers routinely keep partly as an emotional release, and which may contain offensive and emotional remarks — and using that material to analyze the research experience and natural history of the project. Canalized by norms of academic discourse, such material can be of considerable value. But by convention, the scientist has come to embody objectivity and detachment. Involvement in the field is viewed almost as contamination that has to be exorcised by an avoidance of reflection and an aseptic prose style. This has the consequence that a "large area of knowledge is systematically suppressed as 'non-scientific' by the limitations of prevailing research methodologies" (Clarke 1975, p. 96). That area needs to be prized open.

Coming Clean

Yet to a large extent, we get to hear only of successful studies. Failures are rarely written up and analyzed, except via the academic grapevine, despite the fact that they can provide fruitful instructional material. Indeed, it is interesting to record how, only comparatively recently, it was considered academically appropriate for social scientists to abandon the dispassionate and detached image of "science" for descriptions of their personal involvement in the field. One often has the feeling, moreover, that reports on fieldwork experience gloss over the problems, or treat them in a semi-comical manner. There is a tendency to hive off the account on methods to "the smooth, methodological appendix" found in many research reports (Bell and Newby 1977, p. 63) which can be a requirement of publishers who find such accounts superfluous. Indeed, Whyte (1943, 1955) owes much of his richly deserved reputation for *Street Corner*

Society to his frankness and honesty in discussing his initial stumbling approaches in Cornerville and also to his willingness to speak of his "foolish errors and serious mistakes" (Whyte 1981, p. 359).

And, until he wrote, there simply were not many detailed accounts available on the dilemmas of fieldwork. In fact, Wax (1971, p. 5) recalls that in the 1950s no one even spoke of "participant observation." Since then, serious and insightful material on this area has been published by, among others, Clarke (1975), Polsky (1971), Bohannan (in Smith-Bowen 1964), Wax (1971), Van Maanen (1978), Dalton (1964), Holdaway (1980), Chatterton (1978), Manning (1972), and Liebow (1967). In particular, the student is advised to start with the essential, classic account of Whyte (1955) on his methods in *Street Corner Society*, and then to scrutinize a number of the more general treatments of the method as in Van Maanen (1979), McCall and Simmons (1969), Johnson (1975), Lofland (1971, 1976), Bell and Newby (1972), Schatzman and Strauss (1973), Schwartz and Jacobs (1979), Freilich (1977), Agar (1980), Junker (1960), and Becker (1970). A review of this literature encourages one in the view that a full history of the research process is an essential element in reporting a project because of the light it can shed on the nature of the data. Increasingly, then, people are beginning to appreciate that a truncated, flippant, or anodyne account of the project's development is not sufficient, and that a serious and deep analysis of the research role, and the research project, must form a prominent part of an observational study.

This view gains particular strength in light of the fact that in other styles of research the writer is obliged to parade his data for all to see, and she or he can be criticized on the collection, presentation, and interpretation of the data. In field research, in contrast, we are heavily reliant on the integrity of the researcher in terms of detailing the nature and quantity of observations and interviews, the process of interpreting the data, and the selections made in the report. Normally the field notes are not visible, the interviews are not available at length, and the reasons for selecting quotes or specifying particular incidents are not articulated (Van Maanen 1984). This places a heavy responsibility on the academic integrity of the researcher, and he should come clean not only on the nature of his data — how and where it was collected, how reliable and valid he thinks it is, and what successive interpretations he had placed on it — but also on the nature of his relationship with the field setting and with the "subjects" of the inquiry.

The Research Craft

Yet another reason for doing this is to reveal to students that fieldwork is a *craft*, requiring both tenacity of purpose and competence in a number of social skills. In particular, qualitative research should not be seen as a soft option (the "you can throw any dummy anywhere" approach, as it was called at an American Sociological Association seminar), which only requires one to languish on the nearest nudebeach and to pen a flowery description of the conduct of the "natives." Several accounts of field research, in contrast, touch on the stress, the deep personal involvement, the role-conflicts, the physical and mental effort, the drudgery and discomfort (and even the danger), and the time-consuming nature of observational studies for the researcher. Riecken (1969) for example, who was involved with Festinger in the study of an apocalyptic group (amusingly sent-up in Alison Lurie's novel *Imaginary Friends*, 1967), speaks of frustration, disorientation, and the difficulty of suppressing one's own feelings which, if ventilated, might have damaged the continuance of the research. This implies that the researcher has to learn to sustain relationships with people with whom one normally might not easily mix (as in Fielding's 1982 study of the right wing National Front in Britain), and to exploit his emotional involvement with them for data; for, all the time, one is continually exercising the "most fundamental technique of all — *alleviating suspicion*" (Wax 1971, p. 79; my emphasis). In essence, one has to learn how to inveigle one's way into the life of a group, build up contacts with key actors, and retain one's emotional balance continually in order not to spoil acceptance and also to keep on collecting research material.

Surprisingly, a number of key professions do not train their members in essential skills — doctors are often not taught a good "bed-side manner," and detectives are not trained on running informants — so that they learn from adopting the "operational code" as to how things are actually done by colleagues. Much the same is true of qualitative researchers ("like many fieldworkers I went into the field ill prepared, technically and intellectually": Wax 1971, p. 61) who frequently learn the hard way. Occasionally a "school" develops around a powerful personality or a fieldwork tradition develops, as in Chicago before the war or in southern California in the 1970s. But much observational research seems to be the work of soloists, who opportunistically react to a sudden chance and who often enjoy little preparation and little formal training.

But many of the pivotal social skills of fieldwork are, like general social acumen, difficult to transmit and not always easy to apply in specific situations. How does one avoid being captured by marginal figures? How does one *lessen* rapport once established? How does one deflect over-eager but near-useless informants? And how does one prevent oneself slipping over the balance from empathy to "going native"? Reiss (1968) recalls a chilling account of a researcher going over the limit beyond which many of us would, I trust, feel uncomfortable:

> Participant observation can be socialization with a sociological vengeance .... This observer, in a high crime rate negro area, was reported by his fellow observers to have done the following things. In this particular situation [a police station], a common practice when the men in the lock-up called for water was to walk down the row of cells and flush the toilets. The men in the block got the message. One evening, when a prisoner called for water, Mr. M., to the delight of the officers, walked down the block and flushed the toilets. What is more, on the last evening he was in the station, one of the officers said: "Mr. M., what did you learn while you were here this summer?" And Mr. M., to the shock of a fellow observer, replied: "I learned to hate niggers." I even suspect he shocked many of the officers with that. He had become a kind of mockery of what they were. (Reiss 1968, p. 366)

Continued involvement in the field can be likened to being constantly on stage. The role has to be played without dropping your guard, and researchers frequently comment on the strain this causes, not only on themselves but also on their families. In brief, fieldwork is *demanding*, and the researcher is required to perform a role that may be far from easy and can scarcely be learned in advance or by instruction. Evans-Pritchard's anecdote that he was packed off to the bush with the instructions to "keep off the women, take quinine daily, and play it by ear" (Clarke 1975, p. 105) is echoed by Everett Hughes at Chicago, where aspiring fieldworkers were somewhat traumatically pushed out of the nest by him and told to "fly on their own" (Gans 1967, p. 301).

Research Dilemmas

This means that there is a greater element of risk and uncertainty associated with this style of research compared with other methods. Furthermore, the problematic nature of fieldwork is accentuated if we examine a number of dilemmas and setbacks encountered by people during research. Yablonksy (1968) was threatened with violence in a commune, and Thompson (1967) was beaten up by Hell's Angels; Schwarz (1964) was attacked verbally and physically during his study in a mental hospital, where he was seen as a "spy" by both patients and staff; and Vidich and Bensman (1958, 1968) were caricatured in a Fourth of July procession in the town they had studied by an effigy bending over a manure-spreader. And if the early anthropologists risked dysentery from drinking polluted water — I await the first obituary in an academic journal recounting the career of a researcher felled by AIDS — then contemporary researchers can face the formidable hazards of the law. Braithwaite's (1985, p. 136) study of corporate crime was delayed for two years by lawyers representing the managers he had interviewed and he was forced to answer 300 empirical claims that might be raised in court. These examples could be multiplied by horror stories gleaned from the academic circuit, where tales abound of obstructionist gatekeepers, vacillating sponsors, factionalism in the field setting forcing the researcher to choose sides, organizational resistance, respondents subverting the research role, sexual shenanigans, and disputes about publication and the veracity of findings. Such pitfalls and predicaments can rarely be anticipated, yet they may fundamentally alter the whole nature and purpose of the research.

It would be instructive if we possessed a readily available body of knowledge on this area. This could provide both guidelines for students and others and a focus for analytical comment on the nature of these obstacles which can painfully impale the unwitting researcher. Understandably, for career and status reasons, there may be a reluctance to divulge too much of one's pitfalls, but even erstwhile attempts to deal with actual research dilemmas can founder on unexpected hazards. Authentic and candid accounts of the backstage story of research projects are few and far between (with Whyte 1981, p. 359) reflecting in the 1950s that "it seemed as if the academic world had imposed a conspiracy of silence regarding the personal experiences of fieldworkers." There is Hammond's (1964) *Sociologist at Work*, which stands out as a milestone. Nevertheless, it contained only one article on the researcher's response to fieldwork experience. This is more than Lazarsfeld and Rosenberg's (1955) standard textbook of the 1950s on methods, which ignored participant observation on the grounds that there were no systematic analyses of its methodology (while of 36 articles in Denzin's, 1970, collection, only 3 dealt with observation: Clarke 1975, p. 102). In an interesting analysis of the Hammond collection, Baldamus (1972, pp. 289, 295) comments on the "highly insecure, frequently trivial, and unaccountably erratic descriptions of their unofficial methods," while he surmises that much "remains hidden away in notebooks, research files, and preliminary drafts."

Politics of Research

In short, one feels that much is left unsaid and that there are restraints on being completely open. For instance, an attempt to produce a British counterpart to Hammond ran into a number of problems which illustrate graphically the difficulties of writing frankly and "honestly" about what actually happens before, during, and after research. Ironically, Colin Bell, one of the editors of the volume, *Doing Sociological Research* (Bell and Newby 1977), discovered that his willingness to expose his views on the "tensions, conflicts, animosities, jealousies and later recriminations" surrounding a community study (of Banbury in Oxfordshire) led to a threat of legal action from his former colleagues in the research team (Bell 1977). That raises particularly the issue of libel laws in Britain which, along with the Official Secrets Act (covering especially research on defense, prisons, police, etc.), are enough to petrify any publisher's lawyer into fighting shy of contentious material. This reaction is more than likely when dealing with relatively low-sale, low-profit academic works (no *cause célèbre* battle in the courts à la "Lady Chatterley" for a book on methodology, I'm afraid).

Indeed, one chapter in Bell and Newby's collection had to be withdrawn on legal advice (it happened to be *my* contribution), another was almost withdrawn, and several contributions state explicitly that they felt forced to dilute and restrain their accounts. Intriguingly, then, even a serious academic endeavor to "tell it like it really is" has to back-peddle, leaving a feeling that far more could be told about the concealed micropolitics of research. Frustrating as it may be, we simply have to face up to the fact that, institutionally, it proves difficult for social scientists to be totally open about their research experience (Van Maanen 1984).

Perhaps we should even be wary of the status of accounts on research, for they themselves are none other than one particular version of events. They may well be in convincing "confessional" style (as opposed to "didactic deadpan": Watkins 1963), but they are nevertheless bowdlerized, post hoc interpretations polished up for academic presentation. However, they can serve to highlight a number of salient issues related to this area. In particular, the Bell and Newby collection illuminates the special dilemmas for British researchers, in terms of libel laws and the centralized control of access and funding in government ministries, which are in some respects less acute in North America. For example, Cohen and Taylor (1977) used their position as teachers in a maximum security prison to develop research on the inmates. Once they wished to formalize this project in terms of funding and publication, however, they encountered the power of the central government Home Office in London, which (armed with the Official Secrets Act) subjected them to "years of fruitless negotiation," restricted their access, imposed intolerable delays, demanded censorship of basic material, and withheld information on policy developments of vital concern to the research. This left them with a feeling of "total cynicism."

Now a radical sociologist or criminologist would argue that this episode merely demonstrates the bad faith of the watchdogs for the "repressive state apparatus," and that the rejection itself is the real revelation about the system. But this is small consolation to young researchers who wish to get into the field and need to publish to secure their careers. In a sense, total cynicism is a luxury for those who have already made it, or who simply do not care anymore; for simply to detail the battles with gatekeepers is usually to entail permanent banishment. It is a fact of life that in many European countries research in areas likely to illuminate aspects of local or central government policy or performance is "political" in an ideological and even party political sense. The decentralized nature of local and state jurisdictions in North American society has advantages for access, in that a refusal in one state does not preclude access in another state, whereas in Britain, for instance, the red light from a ministerial watchdog agency usually means "finito." One tends to agree with Becker that, culturally, the United States "is fortunate in having fewer barriers, in the form of closed social circles and rules against interaction outside of them, than most societies" (Becker 1970, p. 70).

To a certain extent, these bones of contention arise in areas where politically sensitive issues are exposed by research whose topicality guarantees attention in the media and which can lead to pressure on policy-makers, spokespersons for agencies, and politicians. Research on race, crime, drugs, and social services may be picked up and "distorted" by media in discomforting ways (Morgan 1972). Closed social groups can also react in a hostile fashion to research findings (minor scandals surrounded research on "Middletown," "Yankee City," and the TVA: Vidich and Bensman 1968, p. xiii). In a fairly extreme example, Wallis (1977) focuses on the moral and political problems encountered in his research on Scientology, which almost led to his account being withdrawn from publication. He observes that "research on human subjects perennially poses moral and political dilemmas, the diversity and acuteness of which are only rarely matched in the natural sciences." In his case, he encountered a staff member of the Scientology organization who posed as a student to enter his classes (and you cannot get a clearer indication of determination than that!); forged letters arrived intimating that Wallis had been engaged in a homosexual love affair and had spied for the Drug Squad (letters were also sent to his university); an article of his on this harassment led to threats of legal action and to complaints to his funding body (the SSRC) about *his* "unethical" conduct; and publication became a long-drawn out hassle. With an expensive Queen's Counsel in the wings to advise the Scientologists on libel, over one hundred amendments were forced on the published version of the dissertation. There was too a right of rejoinder for the Scientologists which was published as an appendix to Wallis' book (1976).

Now, clearly, this hostility to research and sensitivity to publication is itself of importance in evaluating Scientology. One may even exult, when things go wrong, at the thought of having juicy "war stories" to tell (Van Maanen 1984). But I suspect that that was little comfort to Wallis at the time. Publishers, for instance, require that authors indemnify them in the event of costs arising from libel actions (which are prohibitively expensive in Britain), meaning that authors cannot afford to contemplate legal redress (even if they feel confident of winning). Even so, most British publishers panic at the merest whiff of a writ. The academic, desperately wishing to publish, is in a weak position, and such prolonged and intricate affairs can make him or her feel deeply isolated and thoroughly miserable. And the story does not end with publication, even if it gets that far, as the threat continues to hang over the researcher's head should he fully detail all the personal and institutional machinations involved in the struggle. There are a number of candid accounts of the politics of research, but often these are tempered with remarks that indicate that restraint had to be exercised, that some matters are best left unsaid, and that certain issues had to be dealt with delicately. It is irritating and frustrating not to have complete data on these matters, particularly in relation to the constraints imposed on the research methods.

Factors Influencing Outcomes

Our frustration is generated not merely by unsated curiosity, but far more fundamentally by an intellectual desire to pinpoint the gamut of personal and structural factors that influence the conduct and outcomes of research. Without pretending to be exhaustive, it is possible to focus on a number of features that are not always articulated but can materially influence fieldwork.

First, the personality of the researcher helps to determine his or her selection of topics, intellectual approach, and ability in the field (Clarke 1975, p. 104). But often we are left in the dark as to the personal and intellectual path that lead sociologists to drop one line of inquiry or to pursue another topic. We require more intellectual autobiographies to clarify why academics end up studying what they do. One simple factor, for instance, that is often glossed over in terms of selecting topics and field settings, is geographic proximity. There may be something romantic about Evans-Pritchard, Malinowski, and Boas setting off stoically into the bush, where they lived in relative isolation and virtuous celibacy, but some researchers just pop conveniently down the road to the nearest commune, mental hospital, or topless joint (the latter being doubtless easier in southern California, or Amsterdam, than in the less temperate parts of rural America). They then endeavor to justify the choice on some spurious theoretical grounds.

Second, the nature of the research object — be it a community, a formal organization, or an informal group — is of significance for access, research bargains, and the likelihood of polarity and conflict in the research setting. The reputation of one's institutional background can be of considerable importance (the University of California at Berkeley in the late 1960s, for example, was not exactly a creditable launching pad for research on the justice system: Skolnick 1975, p. 253). The backing of prestigious academic institutions and figureheads may be vital to access in some settings but irrelevant, or even harmful, in others. Platt (1976, p. 45) records a case in Britain where researchers were able to get a member of Parliament to organize a speech in the House of Commons which led to doors being opened.

Third, gatekeepers can be crucial in terms of access and funding (Argyris 1969). The determination of some watchdogs to protect their institution may, ironically, be almost inversely related to the willingness of members to accept research. As Klein (1976, p. 225) remarks, "Social science is not engaged by 'industry' or organizations, but by individuals in gatekeeping or sponsorship or client roles. The outcome, therefore, is also mediated through the needs, resources, and roles of such individuals." Researchers may suffer by being seen continually as extensions of their political sponsors within the setting despite their denials to the contrary. Furthermore, gatekeepers need not only be construed in terms of government agencies and corporate representatives but can also be found in scientific funding bodies, publishers, and within academia. The intellectual development of the discipline, academic imperialism, the institutional division of labor, the selection and availability of specific supervisors, backstage bargaining, pre-contract lobbying, depart-mental distribution of perks (research assistance, travel money, typing support), and patronage can all play a role in determining the status of, and resources for, field research and in specifying why some projects are launched and others are buried (Dingwall et al. 1980; Sharrock and Anderson 1980).

Fourth, the impact that the presence of researchers has on the setting is related to the status and visibility of the fieldworkers. The "lone wolf" often requires no funding, gains easy access, and melts away into the field. The "hired hand," in contrast, may come with a team of people, be highly visible, be tied to contractual obligations, and be expected to deliver the goods within a specified period of time (Wycoff and Kelling 1978).

Fifth, a feature of research that has rarely been examined is the variety of expectations and roles in *team* research that can hinder behavior in the field and lead to conflict about outcomes. Academics in general, and social scientists in particular, probably make poor supervisors. Yet in team research, leadership, supervision, discipline, morale, status, salaries, career prospects, and the intellectual division of labor can promote unexpected tensions in the field and lead to disputes about publication. "Ripping and running" occurs not only among street addicts but also academia, where juniors may fear that a senior researcher will prematurely publish to increase his academic status while cynically exploiting their data, spoiling the field, and ruining their chances of collecting separate data for a dissertation. A love affair breaking up between team members can also spell disaster and undermine time-tables and deadlines. Workloads, ownership of data, rights of publication, and career and status issues are all affected by the constraints of team research. The structural and status frustrations of the hired hand (particularly the temporary research assistant abandoned to the field) may mean that he or she suffers from poor morale, demands much attention from supervisors, becomes estranged from the parent organization, is strongly tempted towards cooptation, becomes secretive towards supervisors, and is a "bother," requiring "unusally intense and patient supervision" (Florez and Kelling 1979, p. 12).

Sixth, the actual conduct of research and success in the field can be affected by a myriad of factors including age, sex, status, ethnic background, over-identification, rejection, factionalism, bureaucra-tic obstacles, accidents, and good fortune. But, again, we rarely hear of failures, although Diamond (1964) recounts how he was ejected from the field in Nigeria, and Clarke (1975, p. 106) speaks of fieldworkers who went insane, panicked, or got cold feet and never even went out to the field — "but we are systematically denied public information on what happens." Observational studies are often associated with young people (graduate students, research assistants), and some settings may require a youthful appearance and even physical stamina (as in Riemer's 1979 study of construction workers). Gender closes some avenues of inquiry but clearly opens up others (Martin 1980). In masculine worlds the female researcher may have to adopt various ploys to deal with prejudice, sexual innuendo, and unwelcome advances (Hunt 1984). And occasionally one hears catty remarks at conferences about women who used their bodies to gain access to information in the field (an accusation that could be applied with equal force to men, but never is). A young student may be perceived as non-threatening and even elicit a considerable measure of sympathy from respondents. But rather than concluding that fieldwork is not for the "over-forties," one could also argue that advancing age and increased status can open doors to fruitful areas of inquiry, such as senior management in business. Personality, appearance, and luck may all play a role in exploiting unexpected avenues or overcoming unanticipated obstacles in the field.

Seventh, a harmonious relationship in the field may come unstuck at the moment of writing and impending publication when the researcher's material appears in cold print. The subjects of research suddenly see themselves summarized and interpreted in ways that may grate with their own partial perspective on the natural setting. Where the research bargain includes an implicit or explicit obligation to consult the group or institution on publication, then severe differences of opinion can arise. These may be almost completely unanticipated, in the sense that it is difficult to predict what organizational representatives will find objectionable (Burns 1977). The study by Vidich and Bensman (1958, 1968) of "Springdale" provoked a scandalized reaction that raised fundamental issues related to invasion of privacy, the ethics of research (on identity, harm, ownership of data etc.), and responsibilities to Cornell University, which had sponsored the research (and which proved unduly sensitive to the outcry from the community). There were also protests from other *academics*. Progressive and radical institutions, highly critical of the establishment and ideologically committed to openness and publication, may themselves be highly sensitive to criticism because of their marginality, susceptibility to discrediting, and desire for legitimacy (as in the case of Dartington Hall School; cf. Chapter 3).

This connects with my eighth, and final, category: namely, the social and moral obligations that are generated by fieldwork. This issue will form a major plank of this work and can be viewed as having two central parts. On the one hand, there is the nature of the researcher's personal relationship with people he encounters in the field. On the other hand, there are the moral and ethical aspects related to the purpose and conduct of research. Briefly, how far can the researcher go in sharing the experience of "deviant" groups without breaking legal and moral codes? How honest should he be about his intentions? How unscrupulous can he be about exposing "reprehensible" institutions? And is his role radically different from the "investigative" journalist? These are profound matters indeed, which have considerable consequences not just for the subjects of research and for the possibility of blocking further access to institutions, but even for the image of our particular discipline.

Obligations

Social science, for example, attracts social and political "liberals" to its ranks, undermines accepted assumptions, demystifies institutions, and can be viewed as subversive. Leading social scientists (including Erving Goffman in his "Presidential Address" to the ASA in 1981) have spoken of an oppositional ideology and of unmasking the forces of power and oppression. Becker (1970, p. 113) encourages us to take sides and maintains that good research will always make some people angry. That makes me think not so much "how angry are they?" but more, "how powerful are they and are they getting closer?"

There is a danger that academic exposures will weaken the standing of particular disciplines and close doors for research. It is painfully obvious, for instance, that researchers have rarely penetrated to the territory of the "powerful," and that many field studies focus on lowly, marginal groups (the so-called "nuts and sluts") which do not go about imposing formal restrictions on the researchers' role and on publication. It is a moot question as to whether the investigation of "the stripper, dwarves, prostitutes, check forgers, the maimed, the blind, the stuttering, and the thief" (Rock 1979, p. 213) really brings us closer to studying the corridors of power. One tactic is to set out to expose the powerful by deliberately employing deception or even disguise, as in the journalist Walraff's (1979) infiltration of several German institutions, and by concealing one's purpose. Another tactic is to accept the institution to be investigated as legitimate, with reservations, and openly to seek access through the formal channels with all the mazes and obstacles of research proposals, control of research funds, gatekeepers, and rights of approval for publication.

There are moral and ideological issues here that individual researchers need to resolve (is it possible to "take the money and run," endeavoring to do good research with "tainted" funds, or are some institutions totally beyond the academic pale?). Sociology, for example, is currently in a rather precarious state (Short 1980; Bottomore et al. 1980), both intellectually and in terms of contraction of numbers and resources, and is in many respects on the defensive. Advocates of observational studies and of interactionism, furthermore, are something of a peripheral segment (Rock 1979); to a certain extent the status and future of disciplines are intertwined with the possibilities for research, in terms of funding and approval from institutional figureheads; and this in turn percolates through to the proponents of field studies.

On the one hand, the politics of research is related to the state, the allocation of scarce resources, and long-term institutional change within higher education. On the other hand, this has profound implications for the precarious, marginal group of fieldwork enthusiasts. A "subversive" sociology, for instance, can rebound not only on the discipline but also on the lone ethnographer knocking on the door of a hospital or a welfare agency. Surely we cannot be content with a sub-discipline that casts its eyes permanently downwards? Yet to approach powerful and prestigious institutions inevitably involves the academic in the compromises and frustrations associated with the politics, and morals, of research.

The Need for Analytical Reflection

Finally, it is possible to be overly erudite and abstruse about the theoretical and methodological underpinnings of observational studies. One can, alternatively, strive for a practical manual of instructions for the intending fieldworker. The former is not the province of this volume, and the latter is something of a futile exercise in that instructions to fieldworkers are often contradictory. This is because observational research involves an inexhaustible variety of settings and an endless range of situational exigencies for which ready-made recipes do not exist. The conduct of the researcher, and the outcomes of research, are vulnerable to unique developments in the field and to dramatic predicaments that can often be solved only *situationally*. Paradoxically, we must try to learn from our mistakes, but that cannot prevent us repeating them.

This can only be a source of irritation for those who hold that the research process must be a controlled, detached, and formalized set of procedures. Within the ranks of qualitative researchers too there are different models of research, the research role, and the ethical dilemmas of research. For example, at an ASA seminar on field methods, John Lofland held out a highly professional model of virtually certificating researchers, demanding high standards of performance (with fifteen pages of single-spaced notes per hour of observation as a norm for students), and arguing for the protecting of the field from incompetents. Obviously, there is a great deal of sense in this approach, for "smash-and-grab" ethnographers can destroy opportunities for future research, and inadequately trained researchers can wreak havoc in the field. But perhaps there is a danger of making observational research a protected, esoteric, and even self-consciously elitist activity.

An alternative approach is to encourage students and young academics to indulge their intellectual curiosity and youthful enthusiasm when given the chance to enter the field. There are two models juggling for attention here: the trained, skillful, well-prepared, and responsible professional, and the enthusiastic amateur. I do not wish to draw some false dichotomy here, and certainly do not want to advocate intellectual backwoodsmanship, in which lack of preparation and expertise is somehow seen as a morally superior state likely to secure magical success. But the former approach, however laudatory, does tend to exclusiveness and to closing avenues of inquiry; whereas the latter view does keep open the possibility of utilizing personal life experiences, and serendipitous opportunities, for producing sociological data (as in the cases of Becker 1963, Polsky 1971, Ditton 1977 and Roth 1963 on jazz musicians, hustlers, bread salesmen, and a tuberculosis ward, respectively). To a great extent, I would support Becker's feeling that students should be stimulated to simply "get in there and see what is going on" (Atkinson 1977, p. 32).

This position is based on a personal preference for a social science that remains in touch with concrete social experience in a "natural" setting, and one in which young academics cut their teeth on empirical research involving contact with people and with various forms of data (getting "the seats of their pants dirty with *real* research," as Park told his Chicago classes: Burgess 1982, p. 6). I can imagine that some students and some supervisors, for career and publication reasons, avoid fieldwork because it is time-consuming, risky, and unpredictable and plump for research with more formal, predictable, and structured methods. This opens up the dangerous prospect of academics being mesmerized by the "fetishism of numeracy" and divorced from an emphasis on social process and from an accent on field research (Cain and Finch 1980).

Above all, we would do well to recall Mills' (1959) trenchant and still pertinent warning to avoid the twin dangers of abstracted empiricism and grand theory. In contrast, I remain an unrepentant advocate of qualitative field research precisely because it is vulnerable to unexpected hindrances and opportunities. These can be compensated for by the possibility that it has a greater chance than with more structured research to produce fresh, insightful, readable, graphic, and moving material. The overriding attraction of fieldwork, in short, is that it constitutes an "exploration into unexplored territory" (Whyte 1955, p. 357).

A crucial part of that exploration involves analytical reflection on the moral and political dilemmas of fieldwork. For the observational method is suffused with irreducible ambivalence that may cause such emotional and intellectual confusion in the researcher that he or she abandons the field, refuses to write up the data, or becomes converted and ceases to investigate altogether (like the two observers who attended an evangelistic crusade meeting and "saw the light").

The social-psychological impulse that drove the academic into the field in the first place may contain an existential, convoluted element of using research as a "vehicle for entering reality" and as a search for authenticity (Rock 1979, p. 184). In practice, that reality may evade description, the research process may seem almost fraudulent and even predatory, and the attempt to experience membership at first-hand may become self-defeating. Paradoxically, the genuinely sensitive fieldworker may come to feel that the research experience is untranslatable, and that even reflecting on it somehow betrays the intimacy and irreducibility of the direct involvement with other human beings.

But sober reflection is essential to a credible scientific enterprise. It seems incumbent, then, on mature fieldworkers to reflect on the dynamics of the micropolitics and interactional ethics of research in order to canalize the selective "war stories" that inform the largely oral tradition in this area (Van Maanen 1984) into a body of knowledge available for analysis and instruction. A sophisticated and self-critical reflection on the nature of the research enterprise should, in my opinion, not only serve to strengthen and illuminate the foundations of the craft tradition in fieldwork, but also help to shed light on the social, moral, and political processes through which social science gets conducted.

2. ETHICAL CONSIDERATIONS IN FIELDWORK

Through his research tactics Humphreys reinforces an image already prevalent in some circles that social scientists are sly tricksters who are not to be trusted .... Social research involving deception and manipulation ultimately helps produce a society of cynics, liars and manipulators, and undermines the trust which is essential to a just social order. (Donald Warwick, in Bulmer 1982, p. 58)

The use of covert methods reflects the nature of social reality. Sneaky and deceptive methods are necessary to do good social science because social order rests on deceitfulness, evasiveness, secrecy, frontwork, and basic social conflicts. Secrecy and deceit are particular characteristics of the centres of power in society: in order to penetrate these, secrecy to outsiders must be matched by deception to get in. (Donald Warwick and Jack Douglas, in Bulmer 1982, pp. 58, 226)

Introduction

The view that science is neutral and beneficial evaporated in the wake of the Nuremburg trials (detailing the Nazis' "medical experiments" in concentration camps) and in the horrifying aftermath of the atomic bombs dropped on Japan in 1945. Controlling science, however, raises acute practical, ethical, and legal questions that are difficult to resolve. Those questions confront us with fundamental dilemmas such as the protection of subjects versus the freedom to conduct research and to publish research findings. These issues can be dealt with at various levels — in philosophical debate on ends and means, in terms of a profession's reputation and control of its members, and in the light of the personal predicament of the fieldworker in the research setting.

I shall endeavor to handle these issues in a pragmatic, down-to-earth manner. I am neither a philosopher nor a lawyer (and if there is anything more frightening than the thought of a society run by sociologists, it is the idea of a world regulated by a combination of lawyers *and* philosophers). And that means that I approach this minefield warily. Caution is required not merely because of the depth of the contentious dilemmas involved, but also because there is no unanimity in the academic profession on such matters (as the polar positions of Warwick and Douglas quoted above illustrate).

Here I shall touch on a number of central elements in the ethical debate on research: Are there areas that should not be researched? What dilemmas are raised by work with "deviants"? How persuasive is the "conflict methodology" espoused by Douglas and others? Is fieldwork inevitably interactionally deceitful? And can the academic profession successfully control research via codes and regulations? Then I shall examine some of the concrete issues elicited by ethical reflection on research, including consent, deception, privacy, identification, confidentiality, causing harm, and spoiling the field. Ethical conundrums abound in professional practice (as in law and medicine), in the natural sciences, but perhaps most insistently in the social sciences because of their investigative nature and their concern with human subjects. Surveys, interviews, documentary evidence, and above all, observation raise ethical questions that concern most researchers in the range of social scientific disciplines mentioned in the previous chapter. Again, I wish to clarify that my focus is predominantly sociological and anthropological but that the dilemmas explored are relevant to the other disciplines that employ qualitative methods. Finally, I shall argue a position that is skeptical both of codes and of conflict methodology.

But, first, I shall indicate a number of studies that have given rise to moral and ethical questions. In medical research, for instance, actual physical harm can be done to subjects, as in the Tuskegee syphilis study and in the Willowbrook hepatitis experiment; while patients' rights can be violated, as when live cancer cells were injected beneath the skin of non-consenting geriatrics (Brandt 1978, Barber 1976, Katz 1972). This background is important because, for a number of reasons, the attempt to control bio-medical research and to protect its subjects has also become the model for the social sciences (Reiss 1979). In social sciences frequent reference is made to a number of studies that raised considerable dust on ethical aspects of research. Vidich and Bensman's (1968) revelations about the community "Springdale" caused a furore among the townspeople and fellow academics in relation to identification, harm, sponsorship, and professional ethics. Festinger's membership of a sect (Festinger et al. 1956) involved a measure of deception and also implicit if not explicit affirmation for the group which could scarely be described as "non-directive." In the late 1960s US academics were shocked on discovering CIA involvement in the source of funding for "Project Camelot" (Horowitz 1970). Milgram's (1963) renowned experiment on authority required unwitting subjects to think that they were inducing "pain" to others in a laboratory situation. Disguise and deception have been used in La Pierre's (1934) pioneering study of prejudice when he entered restaurants and hotels accompanied by a Chinese couple and also in studying reactions to aspiring members of Alcoholics Anonymous, where students posed as alcoholics (Lofland

and Lejeune 1960). There is finally the well-known, if not now notorious, research of Laud Humphreys (1970) on homosexuals, whom he covertly observed in a public toilet and later questioned in their homes under the guise of a different project. For details and debate on these studies the reader is referred to three excellent readers by Klockars and O'Connor (1979), Sjoberg (1968), and Bulmer (1982), and to texts dealing with ethical issues in research such as Barnes (1979), Diener and Crandall (1978), Boruch and Cecil (1983), Rynkiewich and Spradley (1976), and special issues of the *American Sociologist* (1978) and *Social Problems* (1973, 1980).

The Issues

One moral position that a social scientist may take is that certain topics are quite beyond the academic pale. A researcher may reject involvement with violent or anti-semitic groups or may avoid projects related to the defence and intelligence establishments. Presumably most of us would not wish to witness torture, to observe a gang rape, or to watch child pornography being filmed. The journalist may feel obliged to do so, either overtly or covertly, whereas the known presence of an academic could be construed as lending validity to the activities in question. Covert research could be conducted by an academic in the interest of exposing the nefarious practices; but, even then, for some social scientists, certain areas are simply taboo because association with them is morally repugnant.

A major difficulty does arise, however, in that standards of what is acceptable may change. One man's meat is another man's moral or ideological poison. A radical sociologist or criminologist, for instance, may be acerbic about the state and avoid funding by it and institutions sponsored by it. To a large extent he will thereby remove himself from most funding opportunities, which directly or indirectly emanate from the state's purse (Klockars 1979, p. 262). But he will also exclude himself from research on prisons, schools, courts, social work, hospitals, the military, the police, and a large number — and wide range — of governmental bureaucracies. That seems to be a heavy, and even self-defeating, academic price to pay.

But there is just no unanimity among researchers on this. I, and others, have researched the police, whereas for some this agency represents the most reprehensible unit in the "repressive state apparatus." For them, the police (along with courts, prisons, and probation) are quite untouchable. Police *are* brutal, racist, and corrupt — and if they were only that they would be irredeemable, and unresearchable: but they are also compassionate, humane, humorous, and even determined *not* to be used for the state's ends.

To stop researching institutions, moreover, is to abdicate any pretension to change them. In brief, while some topics are morally objectionable in the eyes of some social scientists, there is no agreement on precisely what areas should *not* be researched.

Related to this is the peculiar nature of research on "deviants." On the one hand, you can take the position that certain groups, such as violent motorcycle gangs, should not be studied because of their involvement in criminal activities. Here the continued presence of the researcher appears to condone that violence (e.g., what if the group paints swastikas and threats of violence on synagogues?). Indeed, the academic may be obliged to engage directly in illegal activities as part of the research role. On the other hand, should the researcher protect subjects from the authorities by not disclosing information on illicit behavior? Or, in contrast, use that information precisely to expose deviant activities? To a certain extent, the researcher's position is determined by the initial purpose or moral stance taken prior to commencing the research. Does one set out aware of the nature of the group's pursuits, and prepared to accept them morally, or is one self-consciously out to get to the "dirt" and then expose it?

That brings us to "conflict methodology," whose proponents argue that it is the *explicit* purpose of research to expose the powerful and that deception is legitimate. This view has been propagated particularly by Jack Douglas and the San Diego "School" (which Van Maanen 1984, p. 34, refers to as the "West Coast School of Hard Knocks"). There is a strong parallel here with investigative journalism. In Douglas' (1979) view, both academic professional organizations and government wish to repress field methods, professional ethics are "scientific suicide," and basic freedoms are constantly being eroded. Consequently, research should move out of the universities and away from government funding while focusing ineluctably on the powerful. In short, Douglas issues a clarion call for a "subversive" and even anti-government research effort:

> The educated are increasingly joining the mass of smaller business people and skilled workers in their angry opposition to government. By pursuing relentlessly our calling to create new knowledge about human life we can join with them in a defensive guerilla war against the bureaucrats until that day when we can force them to return our basic freedoms. (Douglas 1979, p. 32)

One argument that Douglas and his acolytes employ is that, building on interactionist and ethnomethodological perspectives, ordinary social life is characterized by deceit and impression management. The academic is therefore justified in using techniques based on dissimulation precisely in order to penetrate the "fronts" people use to protect their roles (Bulmer 1982, p. 5). If we ignore for the moment the justification for deceitful means and examine the contention that social relations are regulated via a measure of lies, falsification, and fronts (this view forms a cornerstone of Erving Goffman's work; cf. 1959, 1961, 1972), then there is no reason to expect that fieldwork will be immune from those interactional elements. Ditton (1977, p. 10) sums this up nicely in stating that participant observation is *inevitably* unethical "by virtue of being interactionally deceitful."

Let me illustrate this with a story of a young, inexperienced undergraduate who studied a police organization for a brief period in the Netherlands. She took lodgings in a house where several policemen lived, which enabled her to take part in out-of-work socializing (when asked if she would use information gleaned there for her research, she denied it); in addition, she created sympathy by saying that her supervisor was a slave-driver and she would only get a good grade if she collected negative data on the police. Later, her report was used by superiors to identify police "deviants" whom it was claimed were readily identifiable. This led to a meeting between her and her supervisor and the police, in which her report was described as "lies and falsehood." Then she lied about having to collect negative views when caught between the police and her supervisor. Afterwards, her own colleagues were upset because of closing doors and because of the damage done to the reputation of the profession; they also attacked her for "going native." It is hard to think of what else could have gone wrong. And all this turmoil arose from a three-week field placement by an innocent undergraduate! The police called her a "wolf in sheep's clothing" (van der Poel 1981).

But her predicament illuminates perfectly the situational dilemmas of fieldwork. Unconsciously or semi-consciously, you do "lie through your teeth" (as an experienced American researcher put it at an ASA seminar) and dissemble in order to gain acceptance and to get at the data. To me, these dilemmas and ambivalences are inevitable and irreducible in fieldwork and are virtually impossible to resolve in advance.

A quite different argument is raised when these techniques and tactics are practiced consciously and covertly. For example, Humpreys (1970), in order to study male homosexuals, adopted the role of "watch-queen," which enabled him to serve as lookout and at the same time observe interaction between homosexuals in the rest room. He then recorded the license number of cars and traced men's names and addresses. Later, as part of a "social health survey," he visited these men at home — having changed his hair style, clothes, and car — and interviewed them. In other words, he employed covert observation on a "deviant" group engaged in illicit activity.

Incidentally, Reynolds (1982, p. 198) mentions that there must be few investigators who can claim that "they assisted participants in achieving an orgasm"; my hunch is that, if all fieldworkers "coughed" to all their sins, then Reynolds might well have to alter his opinion substantially. Humprey's use of deception, misrepresentation, and manipulation has been severely criticized for taking advantage of a "relatively powerless group," for damaging the image of social scientists, and for encouraging "sneaky" practices in other parts of society. This has led Warwick (1982) to comment:

> Social scientists have not only a right but an obligation to study controversial and politically sensitive subjects, including homosexuality, even if this brings down the wrath of the public and government officials. But this obligation does not carry with it the right to deceive, exploit, or manipulate people. My concern with backlash centers primarily on the alienation of ordinary individuals by research methods which leave them feeling that they have been cheated, deceived, or used. If social scientists set themselves and their methods above society, then they must be prepared to take the consequences. (Warwick 1982, p. 55)

Some would argue that such conduct is damaging to the academic profession and constitutes a serious infraction of professional ethics. And, in order to protect both subjects and the profession, codes of ethics are drawn up to regulate the conduct of research. A central plank here is that of "informed consent," in which subjects should be aware that they are being investigated. This would seem to ban covert research entirely. If applied strictly, there is a danger that such a code would abolish a great deal of participant observation research while, ironically, serving to protect the powerful.

These issues have raised fundamental debate about the very nature of the academic enterprise and about the relationship between social science and research ethics, bureaucratic protection and secrecy, political control and individual rights and obligations (Wilkins 1979, p. 113). Does the end of knowledge justify the scientific means (Homan and Bulmer 1982, p. 114)? What is public and what is private? When can research be said to be "harming" people? Does the researcher enjoy any immunity from the law when refusing to disclose information? In what way can one institutionalize ethical norms — such as respect, beneficence, and justice (Reiss 1979) — to ensure accountability and responsibility in the use and control of information on human subjects? And to what extent do betrayal of trust, deception, and invasion of privacy damage field relationships, make the researcher cynical and devious, enrage the "participants" in research, harm the reputation of social scientific research, and lead to malpractice in the wider society?

All of these points generate ethical, moral, legal, professional, and practical problems and positions which continue to reverberate at conferences, during discussions, and in print. Rather than arguing the pros and cons of each point here, which is beyond the scope of this book, I intend to examine these issues in terms of a number of practical problems encountered in fieldwork situations that have an ethical component. These are consent (and codes), deception, privacy, identification, confidentiality, and spoiling the field.

Ethical Research Dilemmas

CONSENT AND CODES

There exists an understandable desire to protect vulnerable groups from research (such as "fetuses, children, prisoners, institutionally mentally ill and retarded": Gray 1979, p. 206). Because the rights of such people have been flagrantly violated in the past, particularly in bio-medical research, professional and ethical codes have been developed. These embody principles related to the dignity and privacy of individuals, the avoidance of harm, and the confidentiality of research data. Because social science may focus on lowly and inarticulate groups in society, and because research findings may be utilized by people in positions of power against the interests of those groups, professional codes of ethics have been drawn up (for the ASA see "Footnotes" 1982). These tend to adopt the bio-medical model. Medical research has often been performed on individuals and captive groups in controlled settings. The question is whether or not the assumptions behind regulating such conduct are appropriate to other areas of social science. For instance, the problems of "access, selection, consent, and of risks and benefits" are often not the same for persons as they are for formal organizations (Reiss 1979, p. 67).

In particular, a major element in the ASA code is the concept of "informed consent," by which the subjects of research have the right to be informed that they are being researched and also about the nature of the research. Federal agencies in the United States follow the rule for sponsored research (derived from the National Commission for the Protection of Human Subjects of Biomedical and Behavioral Research) "that the potential research subject understand the intention of the research and sign an 'informed consent' form, which incidentally must specify that the subject may withdraw from the research project at any time" (Weppner 1977, p. 41). Peer review groups in universities monitor the ethical component of contract and other research. The key question here is, to what extent is this appropriate to participant observation research? As Weppner (1977) observes, this threatens the continued existence of much "street-style" ethnography.

Let us say, for instance, that during my research with the police in Amsterdam the patrol car was directed to a fight and the two constables jumped out and started wrestling with the combatants. Was I supposed to step up to this writhing shindig and shout "freeze!" and then, inserting my head between the entangled limbs, whip out my code and, Miranda-like, chant out the rights of the participants? When Powdermaker (1967) came face-to-face with a lynch mob in the deep South, was she supposed to flash an academic identity card at the crowd and coolly outline her presence? In these circumstances gaining consent is quite inappropriate, because activity is taking place that cannot be interrupted. Indeed, to have endeavored to do so in many other situations that I encountered in the field would have effectively destroyed my research.

In a large organization, engaged in constant interaction with a considerable number of clients (including ordinary members of the public, victims, criminals, people in distress, etc.), it is not only physically impossible to inform everyone of one's purpose and identity but also damaging to the research itself. Events were covered that included public ceremonies, vicious rioting, private grief, arrests, interrogation, and incarceration. To have explained my presence would have undermined the opportunity to witness areas normally closed to civilians, because the people involved assumed that I was a plain clothes policeman or at least that I "belonged" with the police (cf. Skolnick 1975). If asked, I explained who I was, but I did not enter into the finer theoretical points of symbolic interactionism with everyone I encountered (while I doubt if a drunken Turkish guestworker or a stoned German junkie were all that interested). In fieldwork there seems to be no way around the predicament that informed consent — divulging one's identity and research purpose to all and sundry — will kill many a project stone dead.

There are simply no easy answers to these situational ethics in fieldwork. For instance, researchers often confess to professional "misdemeanors" while in the field (Wax 1971, p. 168). Malinowski (1967) socked a recalcitrant informant on the jaw; Powdermaker

(1966) ceased to concern herself with the ethics of recording events in Hollywood unknown to the participants; Dalton (1964) fed information on salaries to a secretary in exchange for information on her male friend; and Smith-Bowen (1964) deliberately manipulated the research situation when personal objectivity became impossible for her to maintain. What sanctions should we impose for these breaches of "professional standards"?

The acknowledged doyen of qualitative researchers, Whyte (1955, pp. 333–336), broke the law by "repeating" at elections, engaged in "retrospective falsification," and admits to having violated professional ethics. What should we do with Whyte? Haul him in front of an ethics review committee, strip him of all his honors (striking his name from the list of past presidents of the ASA), and ignominiously drum him out of the profession? That seems a rather severe punishment for honesty.

My position is that a professional code of ethics is beneficial as a *guideline* that alerts researchers to the ethical dimensions of their work, particularly *prior* to entry. With formal organizations and certain communities, where entry has to be negotiated through hierarchical channels, a statement of purpose is normally essential to satisfy gatekeepers. Thereafter it may be *situationally* inappropriate to repeat continually that purpose and to identify oneself. The "subjects" of research in an organization may not even have been consulted by superiors about the presence of a researcher in their midst, and may scarcely be in a position to refuse to cooperate. To negotiate access and consent with everyone would be almost futile, while matters would become absurdly complex if some said "yes" and some said "no." In natural settings involving public behavior, such as watching crowd behavior at a football match or studying avoidance rituals on a crowded pavement, then consent seems superfluous and physically unattainable. Any attempt to achieve it in the latter case would only serve to undermine the behavior one wished to observe.

I am not arguing that the fieldworker should abandon all ethical considerations once he or she has got in but, rather, that informed consent is unworkable in some sorts of observational research. Furthermore, Reiss (1979, pp. 72, 77) notes that consent often serves to *reduce* participation and that, while "definitive evidence is lacking," refusals seem more frequent from high-status, powerful people than from low-status, less powerful individuals. The philosopher might rail at my placing practical handicaps above ethical ideals. But I am seriously concerned that a strict application of the code will restrain and restrict a great deal of informal, innocuous research where students and others study groups and activities that are unproblematic, but where explicitly enforcing consent will make the research role simply untenable.

Indeed, some commentators have raised even more fundamental objections to codes because, paradoxically, they can be seen to protect the powerful rather than the weak. Jack Douglas (1979, p. 31) views professional ethics generally as a "deceit and a snare." He dismisses informed consent as the "first of a long and even more tortuous series of bureaucratic attempts to destroy our freedom of truth-seeking." Wilkins (1979, p. 109) notes astutely that prisoner's rights are rarely a matter of concern to the authorities until someone wants to do research on prisons. In effect, authorities can protect *themselves* under the guise of protecting the subjects. And it is precisely with formal institutions that consent has to be explicit, but, given that they often have "elaborate screening devices," they can deflect research on sensitive issues. This leads Galliher (1982) to contend:

> Is not the failure of sociology to uncover corrupt, illegitimate, covert practices of government or industry because of the supposed prohibitions of professional ethics tantamount to supporting such practices? (Galliher 1982, p. 160)

The code implies an open society, which plainly some people regard as more of a myth than a reality (Lowry 1972), because they believe that the manipulation of information is an increasing problem in modern society (Douglas 1979, p. 31). This has led some academics to argue that some deception is acceptable, particularly when it is directed against groups or institutions that they do not favor. Clearly, informed consent and deception/disguise are directly opposed to one another.

DECEPTION

While doing research in South Africa, van den Berghe concluded:

> "From the outset, I decided that I should have no scruples in deceiving the government ...." The question is, how much honor is proper for the sociologist in studying the membership and organization of what he considers an essentially dishonorable, morally outrageous, and destructive enterprise? (Galliher 1982, p. 159)

> The social researcher is therefore entitled and indeed compelled to adopt covert methods. Social actors employ lies, fraud, deceit, deception, and blackmail in dealings with each other, therefore the social scientist is justified in using them where necessary in order to

achieve the higher objective of scientific truth. (Jack Douglas; quoted in Bulmer 1982, p. 10)

In normal social intercourse a person who is totally honest is unbearable and socially immature. To a certain extent he, or she, *has* to dissemble to protect his or her autonomy and to lubricate relations with others (Reisman, 1979). Someone who is consciously and egoistically mendacious or devious, however, breaks the strong social norm that we should present ourselves to people as we are, and not misrepresent ourselves. In certain professions some "lying" may be acceptable and be seen as beneficial (Bok, 1978), but, generally, someone caught in a lie is discredited. There are, of course, a number of occupations that routinely use lies, disguise, and deception in their daily work, and these include prostitution, policing, espionage, and journalism. The key question is, should social science be among them?

In terms of research, one can think of deception in relation to the research purpose, the researcher's identity, the use of disguise, the nature of the methods, and in terms of broken promises to the researched. Overlying these matters are two related issues of vital significance in determining one's stance. First, are there areas where some measure of deception is justified in gaining data (yet while bearing in mind, and respecting, privacy, harm, identification, and confidentiality)? And, second, are there some institutions which deserve what they get so that devious means are legitimate and, crucially, it is our intention to *expose* them? Many of us may sympathize with van den Berghe's (1968) predicament, and even admire his resolve, but it is debatable as to which institutions in our society can be meaningfully compared with the South African government. Douglas (see above) promulgates this as our academic *duty*, and assumes that an adversary relationship *should* exist between social science and the "establishment":

> Specifically social scientists are seen as having a responsibility to study those institutions or government agencies that are in a position to mistreat the disadvantaged, and if evidence of wrongdoing is discovered on the part of government officials or administrators, it should be publicly disclosed in an effort to discourage future wrongdoings — regardless of any promises made to the public officials to respect confidential information, their anonymity or privacy. (Bulmer 1982, p. 210)

In this light there is a close resemblance between "conflict methodology" and "investigative journalism."

For example, Gunter Wallraff, a German journalist, disguised his identity, altered his appearance, and worked for the magazine *Stern* in order to expose its dubious methods in manufacturing news. He then blew the whistle, although in his case it was more like a fog-horn, and was roundly applauded for so doing (while court actions against him helped considerably to promote his book). Here the specific intention was to expose a particular institution and to identify individuals engaged in practices which some people regard as reprehensible. The story gains its strength precisely because names are named. This conflicts with normal academic convention that the unique identity of persons and organizations should be protected (Reiss 1979, p. 70). I would argue for holding to that convention. But, first, I shall examine a number of studies that have employed some measure of deception.

In a neglected classic on organizational behavior, *Men Who Manage*, Dalton (1959) recounts how he investigated management in a number of firms by working covertly as a manager over a period of years. He used secretaries to gain information, took part in out-of-work socializing to observe the significance of club membership for managers, utilized malcontents for their grievances against the organization, and manipulated intimates as "catalytic agents" to gain data (Dalton 1964). It is difficult to see how Dalton could have obtained the rich wealth of data that he assembled by overt research. In other projects researchers have joined a pentecostal sect as if they were a novitiate (Homan and Bulmer 1982); have undergone plastic surgery, lost weight, altered their age, and adopted a "new personality" in order to study Air Force recruits (Sullivan et al. 1958); and have entered a mental hospital as if they were a patient (Caudill 1958). In other words, researchers have been prepared to use disguise, deception, and dissimulation in order to conduct research. Now the covert–overt distinction is a continuum, rather than a black–white divide, and some elements of covert research ("the betrayal of trust, deception, the invasion of privacy, damage to field relations and the reputation of social research": Homan and Bulmer 1982, p. 121) are not exclusive to covert methods. As such, the questions to be answered are, how far should you go? (in deception) and, should you be concerned with avoiding harm?

For example, I would support Dalton's methods and condone Humphrey's approach in posing as a "watch-queen." But once Humphreys moves to collecting license plate numbers, tracing names, and visiting homes under the guise of a different project, then that represents both a severe invasion of privacy and also a potentially dangerous situation if his data fell into other hands. That is going too far for me. In addition, I was asked for advice by a group of female students in Utrecht who wanted to report to a police station that they had been raped in order to witness policemen's reactions. I objected to this approach on the grounds that making a false complaint is illegal (and might have repercussions for the students); that it would lead policemen to be even more skeptical than they are about academics and research; but principally because it might cause the police to disbelieve the legitimate claims of rape victims (to a greater extent than they already do).

In brief, *some* measure of deception is acceptable in *some* areas where the benefits of knowledge outweigh the harms and where the harms have been minimized by following convention on confidentiality and identity. One need not be always brutally honest, direct, and explicit about one's research purpose. One should not normally engage in disguise. One should not steal documents. One should not directly lie to people and, while one may disguise identity to a certain extent, one should not break promises made to people. Academics, in weighing up the balancing-edge between overt and covert, and between openness and less-than-open, should take into account the consequences for the subjects, the profession, and, not least, for themselves.

I base this position on the moral view that subjects should not be harmed and on the pragmatic perspective that some dissimulation is intrinsic to social life and, therefore, also to fieldwork. Gans (1962) expresses this latter view neatly:

> If the researcher is completely honest with people about his activities, they will try to hide actions and attitudes they consider undesirable, and so will be dishonest. Consequently, the researcher must be dishonest to get honest data. (Gans 1962, p. 46)

The crux of the matter is that some deception, passive or active, enables you to get at data not obtainable by other means. There are frequent references in the literature to fieldworkers as "spies" or "voyeurs" while an experienced researcher advises us to enter the field with a nebulous explanation of our purpose and to be careful that our deception is not found out until after we have left, and states that it is not "ethically necessary, nor methodologically sound, to make known specific hypotheses, background assumptions, or particular areas of interest" (Van Maanen 1978, p. 334). Even in an innocuous study of farm workers in Britain, we find the researcher "coughing" to the following crime: "I was not telling outright lies, but I was engaging in systematic concealment" (Newby 1977, p. 118).

But this does not hold when the primary purpose of the research is to expose people and institutions. This is an extremely knotty area, because some academics argue precisely that researchers should be concerned with documenting abuses in public and business life. This is because they feel that convention on privacy, harm, and confidentiality should be waived when an institution is seen to be evading its public accountability. Holdaway (1980) takes this position on the police in justifying his own covert role (when he worked as a sergeant in London while collecting material for a dissertation):

> The argument that all individuals have a right to privacy, that is to say freedom from observation, investigation and subsequent publication based on the investigation, is strong but it should be qualified when applied to the police .... The police are said to be accountable to the rule of law, a constitutional feature which restricts their right to privacy, but which they neutralise by the maintenance of a protective occupational culture. When such an institution is highly secretive and protective, its members restrict any right to privacy they already have. It is crucial that they are researched .... The covert researcher of the police has to be reminded that he is working within an extremely powerful organization which requires that its public and private practice be revealed on the basis of first-hand observation. (Holdaway 1980, p. 324)

This view is echoed by Marx (1980, p. 41), who suggests that perhaps different standards apply with respect to "deception, privacy, informed consent, and avoiding harm" to the researched against organizations that themselves engage in "deceitful, coercive and illegal activities" and are publicly accountable. Can we salve our academic conscience by arguing that the police comprises such an institution and deserves what it gets? And does that apply to welfare agencies or corporations or state bureaucracies?

If one is not careful, then, one ends with a sort of reverse pride in breaking professional codes, zealously arguing that it is genuinely "ethical" to break norms of privacy for institutions that, one claims, should be more "accountable." There seems to be no answer to this issue, because it is impossible to establish a priori which institutions are "pernicious." One could visualize endless and fruitless debate as to which organizations should be included, particularly as many public bureaucracies of a mundane sort are secretive and protective. The argument that they are also accountable is a telling one. But using covert research methods against them is only likely to close doors rather than to open them. The balance on this matter is ultimately a question for the individual researcher and his or her conscience in relation to feelings of responsibility to the profession and to "subjects." And it seems to be somewhat specious that academics can employ deception with high moral purpose against those that they accuse of deception. This will certainly lead more people to conclude that "Sociology, in short, is not nice" (Fielding 1982, p. 90).

It is interesting, and even ironic, that social scientists espouse some of the techniques normally associated with morally polluted professions, such as policing and spying, and enjoy some of the moral ambivalence surrounding those occupations. The ironies and ambivalences are magnified when researchers study "deviants" and run the danger of what Klockars (1979, p. 269) calls getting "dirty hands." In getting at the dirt one may get dirty oneself (Marx 1980, p. 27). In entering polluted areas, the "back" region where "trade secrets" may be exposed (Goffman, 1959), the researcher faces moral dilemmas related both to involvement in the practices and to exposing the wrongdoing observed. Klockars (1979, p. 275) is clear on this; in research on deviants, the academic promises *not* to blow the whistle and maintains "the immediate, morally unquestionable, and compelling good end of keeping one's promise to one's subjects." His argument is that you must be prepared to get your hands dirty; but also that the researcher protects himself by approaching subjects as "decent human beings," and by engaging in *talk*.

By discussing moral dilemmas openly within his profession, the researcher can avoid the danger of concealing dirty means for "good" ends. Here I would fully support Klockars' (1979) standpoint:

> The implication for fieldwork is to be most wary of any and all attempts to fashion rules and regulations, general guidelines, codes of ethics, or standards of professional conduct which would allow well-meaning bureaucrats and concerned colleagues to mobilize punishments for morally dubious behavior. Doing so will, I think, only have the effect of forcing decent fieldworkers to lie, deceive, wear masks, mispresent themselves, hide the methods of their work, and otherwise dirty their hands more than their vocation now makes morally necessary. (Klockars 1979, p. 279)

In short, my position is to reject "conflict methodology" as a generally inappropriate model for social science. At the same time, I would accept some moderate measure of field-related deception, provided the interests of the subjects are protected — and provided, above all, that it produces good research!

A number of academics, however, do take a very strong line on this area. The claim of Douglas that basically "anything goes" is firmly opposed by Kai Ericson (in Bulmer 1982). Among others, he argues that it is unethical deliberately to misrepresent our identity to gain entry into private domains otherwise denied to us. It is also unethical to misrepresent deliberately the character of our research. Bulmer (1982, p. 217) supports the contention that the use of covert observation as a method is "neither ethically justified, nor practically necessary, nor in the best interests of sociology as an academic pursuit." This does not mean that it is *never* justified, but "its use requires most careful consideration in the light of ethical and practical considerations." Bulmer (1982) then goes on usefully to summarize his position in this debate by arguing that the rights of subjects override the rights of science; that anonymity and confidentiality are necessary but not sufficient for subjects of research (we cannot predict the consequences of publication); and that covert observation is harmful to subjects, researcher, and the discipline. He adds that the need for covert research is exaggerated and more attention should be paid to access as "overt insider"; "covert outsider" is less reprehensible than "convert insider and masquerading as a true participant." And, finally, sociologists should look outside their own profession for ethical guidance and should carefully consider the ethical implications of research before embarking on it. Much of this is sound advice, but it does mean closing avenues to certain types of research. And who is to perform the moral calculus that tells us what to research and what to leave alone?

PRIVACY, HARM, IDENTIFICATION, CONFIDENTIALITY, AND SPOILING THE FIELD

Conventional practice and ethical codes espouse the view that various safeguards should protect the privacy and identity of research subjects. As Bulmer (1982, p. 225) puts it, "Identities, locations of individuals and places are concealed in published results, data collected are held in anonymized form, and all data are kept securely confidential." There is a degree of overlap here with the previous section because some academics argue that these safeguards do not always apply to "public" figures. For example, Galliher draws up an alternative code that *reverses* some of the ASA Ethical Code assumptions and proposals:

Rule 3. When actors become involved in government and business or other organizations where they are accountable to the public, no right of privacy applies to conduct in such roles .... Rule 5. The revelation of wrongdoing in positions of public trust shall not be deemed "confidential information" within the meaning of this rule. (Galliher 1982, p. 162)

This raises two issues: first, What obligations does the researcher have to the researched? and, second, To what extent can public figures claim the same rights of privacy as ordinary citizens?

In general, there is a strong feeling among fieldworkers that settings and respondents should not be identifiable in print and that they should not suffer harm or embarrassment as a consequence of the research. There are powerful arguments for respecting persons (cf. the "Belmont Report" on ethical principles governing research, discussed in O'Connor 1979) and their dignity, and also for not invading their privacy. Exposing people's private domains to academics raises imagery of "Peeping Toms" and "Big Brother" (Mead 1961). It does seem to be going a bit far to lie under beds in order to eavesdrop on conversations (Bulmer 1982, p. 116), but what about attending meetings of Alcoholics Anonymous? If we assume that the research is valuable in clarifying the treatment of alcoholics, that alcoholics are too distressed to worry about someone observing their predicament (their appearance at AA signals their willingness to be open about their problem in the company of others), and that individual identities are preserved, then I see no real problems. I would be far less happy if researchers *posed* as alcoholics, because of the deception played on the members. Yet one could also argue that this is necessary in order to experience the role of an alcoholic seeking aid (and Anderson became a "hobo," while Spradley posed as a vagrant).

To a large extent, I feel that we can become too sensitive on this issue. There is no simple distinction between "public" and "private," while observation in many public and semi-public places is tolerable even when the subjects are not aware of being observed. Some areas are non-problematic, such as observing the work of air hostesses while one is traveling; and others may be related to social problems where some benefit may emerge from focusing on the issue (Weppner 1977). O'Connor (1979) would not even accept the latter as legitimate without the consent of the group concerned. Getting into areas where people believe they are in private and free from observation — at home or in a brothel — becomes more risky and delicate. The major safeguard to place against this invasion of privacy is the assurance of confidentiality.

But even such assurances are not watertight, and sociologists themselves "have often flagrantly betrayed confidence, undoing all the work of covers, pseudonyms, and 'eletions'" (Rock 1979). I mentioned earlier the tendency to choose sites close to one's university, and pseudonyms can often be punctured by looking up the researcher's institutional affiliation at the time of the project.

Everyone now knows that "Middletown" was Muncie, Indiana, that "Rainfall West" was Seattle, and that "Westville" was Oakland, California. Holdaway painstakingly uses a pseudonym for his research station but then refers in the bibliography to publications that make it plain that he studied the Metropolitan Police of London. And how do you disguise research conducted in London, New York, or Amsterdam ("Windmill West"?)? In addition, the cloak of anonymity for characters may not work with insiders who can easily locate the individuals concerned — or, what is even worse, can *claim* that they can recognize them when they are, in fact, wrong. Many institutions and public figures are almost impossible to hide, and if they cooperate in research they may have to accept a considerable measure of exposure, particularly if the media picks up on the research.

This makes it sometimes precarious to assert that no harm or embarrassment will come to the researched (Reiss 1979, p. 70). It is extremely difficult to predict what uses one's research will be put to. When Wallis (1977) states that we must not cause "undeserved harm," then who is to define "deserved" and "undeserved" harm? Even people who have cooperated in research may feel hurt or embarrassed when the findings appear in print (cf. the reactions in "Cornerville," i.e. the North End of Boston, to the publication of *Street Corner Society*: Whyte 1955, p. 346). If there has been some element of deception, then these feelings may be laced with an acute sense of betrayal on reading or learning of the publication: "they have been cheated and misled by someone in whom they reposed trust and confidence" (Bulmer 1982, p. 15). Respondents may not be aware at the time of the research that its findings may be published. Graduate students who speak vaguely of a dissertation may not make it clear that this is not just an internal study assignment but also a public document lodged in a library and open to all (Wallis 1977, p. 159). The more "deviant" and secretive the activity, the more likely it is that subjects will fear consequences, and "the single most likely source of harm in social science enquiry is that the disclosure of private knowledge can be damaging" (Reiss 1979, p. 73).

Assurances of confidentiality in relation to interviews and other research material are not protected by law for researchers, and under certain circumstances the government has the authority to compel them to disclose matters of confidence. Ironically, then, the source of protection, the government, can become the agent of harm (Reiss 1979, p. 73). When Polsky (1971, p. 133), for instance, advocates almost full participation in a criminal culture and, further, argues that "the investigator has to decide that when necessary he will 'obstruct justice' or have 'guilty knowledge' or be an accessory before or after the fact, in the full legal sense of those terms," then he opens up the possibility of academics being jailed. This has happened with journalists who refused to reveal their sources in criminal cases (Sagarin and Moneymaker 1979, p. 185). In practice, Reiss (1979, p. 89) asserts that there is little evidence of failures or of harm to subjects of research. But this issue does raise the lack of immunity for researchers and the possibility that academics could be sanctioned and even jailed for honoring their obligation to protect confidential information gleaned during research. Soloway and Walters (1977) conducted research among active heroin addicts and maintain that legally they were in a fairly strong position to refuse to reveal information on the street scene and to protect themselves against accusations that they were accessories to criminal offences. A recent court case has established a limited privilege for scholarly field notes comparable to that enjoyed by journalists in protecting their confidential sources. The case involved a SUNY graduate student and is being appealed, while the right of the researcher to confidentiality of his field notes must be decided "on a case-by-case basis that balances 'societal interest in fostering scholarly research' against 'the public interest in obtaining information about possible criminal activities'" ("Footnotes" 1984). As someone who has often seen the inside of a cell — during my research, I should add — incarceration holds no romantic charm for me whatsoever (although the ethnographic appeal of observing prison from inside is perhaps not without its attraction for the inveterate fieldworker).

One major theme running through the ethical debate on research is that academics should not spoil the field for others. This is reflected among fieldworkers where there are strong norms not to "foul the nest." But given that replications are rare in social science, that fieldworkers continually seek new and more esoteric settings, and that institutions frequently find one piece of research enough, there is a general tendency to hop from topic and topic. This makes spoiling the field less problematic for prospective researchers, who look elsewhere rather than follow in someone's footsteps.

It may well be problematic, however, for the researched. They may be left seething with rage and determined to skin alive the next aspiring ethnographer who seeks access. In fact, I would be curious to know how many of us have actually made it easier for colleagues to gain access to institutions or groups. It is already the case that anthropologists are not welcome in some Third World countries because they are associated with espionage — and a few well published cases of academic "snooping and duping" in American society might also rebound on social scientists. Indeed, one of the most fundamental objections to conflict methodology is that it will effectively close doors to further research. We cannot kick people in the teeth, or elsewhere, and expect them to go on smiling.

Conclusion

In this chapter I have reviewed a number of salient issues related to the ethics of fieldwork. My rejection of both formalized codes and conflict methodology may appear to leave me perching uncomfortably on a moral fence, but I intend to underpin my perspective in the concluding chapter. Obviously, my views are shaped substantially by my own research background, which commenced with a traumatic experience that touched on several key aspects of the politics and ethics of fieldwork. As a young, naive research student I contracted with a school to make a study of its former pupils. I began with an assumption of good faith on the part of the sponsors, and early relationships were amicable and apparently open. As soon as fieldwork commenced, however, and particularly once I started to commit ideas to paper, major differences of opinion emerged that escalated into a battle to complete the research and to get it published.

There are two reasons for analyzing my academic nightmare here. One is that it personalizes the issues raised above, which reveal that, when you are fighting sponsors, and particularly when you witness the dirty tricks they pull on you, then the finer points of professional ethics tend to be shelved in the lonely and largely individual determination to survive and win. And the other reason is that it could happen to almost any fieldworker. Some elements relate specifically to the British scene, but my predicament could arise almost universally. After all, I was not penetrating the Pentagon or infiltrating the Ku-Klux-Klan, but was engaged on an apparently innocuous study of an innocuous institution. The unsuspecting researcher never knows when an ostensibly anodyne project will blow up in his face. What is trivial to us may be of vital concern to the researched.

3. DIALOGUE OF THE DEAF: A CASE OF SPONSORSHIP AND "PUBLICATIO INTERRUPTUS"

A representative of Dartington (in Platt 1976, p. 93) gave his view of me (alias Frank Brown):

at some stage along the line the idea that the research should become a PhD project, and this would help in his academic career, had been injected, and I can't now remember how, and probably the board did agree to his formulation, and if you like innocently wanting of course to help [Frank Brown] personally, but I think very inadvisedly, and not realizing the implications of such approval, because when the PhD in draft was shown us a great deal of exception was taken to it. Frank Brown, of course, for his part said that we didn't like being told the truth about ourselves, whereas we said this is in fact not the truth .... Frank Brown tried very hard to be detached, impartial, objective, whatever the words mean, but underneath it all there was a discernible hostility to [the institution] and what it represented ... he didn't have the knowledge, the background understanding ... to put [the institution] in a meaningful context .... There then was raised the question of academic freedom ... was it right to prevent publication of research in any shape or form? Well, we considered that the spirit of the understanding at the beginning had been that of consultancy to us, and it should be left to us to draw the inferences.

Introduction

Over fifteen years ago I commenced a doctoral project on Dartington Hall School which still haunts me. It not merely turned out to be a particularly difficult study to conduct, but also involved an acrimonious, drawn-out struggle for the control of publication. This was resolved only a decade after the research commenced, with the publication of *Progressive Retreat* (Punch 1977) by Cambridge University Press (hereafter "CUP"). An earlier attempt to reflect on that experience foundered on legal advice, and when the project was described elsewhere the institution went unnamed and I was dubbed "Frank Brown" (Platt 1976). My motivation for writing about the research now is quite simple. The battle over the publication of my findings may constitute the most telling piece of evidence that I gleaned about Dartington.

Here I endeavor to summarize that conflict with Dartington in terms of the political, personal, and moral dimensions of the research process and, in particular, the research "bargain". Hopefully, an appraisal of my personal battle with a difficult project and hostile sponsors may tell us something of general interest about the frustrations of research. For, in signing a contract with the sponsors who financed my research, I put myself in their power, which I naively expected to be employed benignly. When, in my eyes, it was not so used, there evolved a struggle that raised fundamental issues about the rights of sponsors and the freedom of researchers to publish.

In addition, the struggle illuminates other matters, some of which are peculiar to Britain. In British universities, for instance, the postgraduate student is often a victim of "structured neglect" (Rock 1979) and operates very much alone. Furthermore, the libel laws are so stringent that they considerably restrict what can be said in print about people and institutions. And for a non-British audience it is important to bear in mind that the "public" schools in Britain are traditional, *private* boarding schools (like Eton, Harrow, and Winchester), and that a small progressive wing of the private system is represented by schools such as A.S. Neill's "Summerhill," Bertrand Russell's "Telegraph Hill," and Dartington Hall (Skidelsky 1969).

The project serves also as an excellent example of the unforeseen pitfalls of fieldwork that can radically alter original intentions — changing definitions of the situation (related to mutations among the key personalities or internal political shifts) can rebound on the researcher — and of how the research bargain is open to negotiation and alteration at the whim of sponsors. Ironically, in this case two of the leading "gatekeepers" were sociologists, and their behavior does not exactly encourage one to believe that academics in formal positions of authority, exercising control of the research process, act differently from other organizational watchdogs. Moreover, the people researched were articulate, middle-class men and women who did not just passively accept the research but attacked it and interfered with it.

And, although at the time I saw the struggle from my own particular worm's-eye view (which awakens imagery that doubtless Dartington shares of me), I now see the battle far more in terms of the morality of research, of obligations to the researched, and of the "bad faith" of sponsors. For, clearly, misunderstandings and mistrust complicated communication, and it was difficult to unravel who was being devious, manipulative, and unscrupulous (and when). Should the researcher, for instance, continue to act honorably even when he believes the other side is "screwing" him?

Finally, and most importantly, the reaction of a sponsoring organization when confronted with an outsider's version of its aims and activities may constitute important evidence about the sponsor's self-perceptions and "real," as opposed to espoused, values. In this light, it may well be that I have to propose the somewhat galling premise that my conflict with the sponsors is more revealing about them than the actual research findings.

Dramatis Personae

THE SPONSORS: DARTINGTON HALL

Leonard Elmhirst (1893–1973) was a Yorkshireman who, while studying at Cornell University in the 1920s, met and married a wealthy American widow, Dorothy Whitney Straight (1887–1968). In 1925 they bought an estate in Devon, and in the following year a progessive school was opened there. The estate was a sort of Devonian kibbutz with rural industries, experimental farming, good conditions for the workers, and a rich cultural life. The rural radicalism, which could be mistaken for egalitarianism, barely concealed the fact that two powerful personalities were at the helm who directed practically all operations and who attracted deference as the figureheads of the revamped squirearchy up at "the Hall." The estate had its practical side, its down-to-earth farmers and salesmen; but its ethos was, in practice, high-minded, precious, and introspective. The introspection and the influence of the Elmhirsts can be seen if we briefly examine the Trustees of the Dartington enterprise at the time of the research.

In effect, the Trustees were virtually members of the Elmhirst dynasty. They were a tightly knit group of upper-class intellectual gentry, privately educated, with no participating experience of state education, with a dislike for the traditional "public" school, and with a predilection for progressive education that precluded sending their children to any school but Dartington and that caused three of them to seek their spouse from Dartington and one from another well-known progressive school. And they were mostly well-off. One of them, Michael Young, is one of Britain's best known sociologists of the postwar period. He attended Dartington himself as a pupil, was virtually adopted by the Elmhirsts, and has been a trustee for over twenty-five years. In his career he has been an important innovator and has been engaged in a wide range of educational, sociological, and political roles (including founding the Institute of Community Studies in Bethnal Green, which helped to revive empirical research in British Sociology: Platt 1977). He was to play a key part in the affair.

THE RESEARCHER: MAURICE PUNCH

I was born in 1941 in a blitzed London to Irish, Catholic, working-class parents. Thanks to a grammar school education, I became no longer Irish, Catholic, or working-class. Of such marginal material are sociologists made. It is certainly not possible, or necessary, to attempt an adequate autobiographical sketch here except to hint that some of the research problems may have come from a clash of personalities and temperaments. My home background, for example, was not a conspicuously cultivated one. My incessant reading was frowned upon, and my prolonged studies were never considered respectable "work." The piety — with its Sacred Heart emblems, holy water founts, and rosary beads — was laced with a certain vulgar humor. As a family, we went to church twice on Sundays, ate bacon and cabbage on Saturdays, never tasted spaghetti, curry, or any foreign dish, and were neglectful of the arts and the finer things in life. We spoke of Ireland as "home" and pilloried the English as mean, humorless, and hypocritical.

In late adolescence (a stage I have yet to abandon) I was self-conscious, inhibited, temperamental, and aggressive, and there were frequent clashes with authority. Temperamentally, I felt unsuited for the tedium and pretensions of academic life, but I wanted to achieve status and an academic career appeared to promise this, while allowing me a great deal of personal freedom. I felt that I was more intuitive and creative than my painstaking colleagues (pious functionalists or virtuous statisticians to a man) and, in my written work, I tried to go for humor, irony, iconoclasm, and broad generalizations rather than for stilted, academic prose. My academic contemporaries of the mid-1960s tended to be good bourgeois stock, guiltily fixated on studying the working-class, whereas I was ex-working-class and engaged in scrutinizing the exotic educational institutions of the upper-middle class. Perhaps in projects which are not simply routine and harmonious such biographical details might be elucidated to explain difficulties or failure.

But such details are largely imponderable, and we are dependent upon what people are prepared to reveal about themselves. However, people better able to judge than the protagonists might discern in this case that the cultural and social differences between researcher and researched provided one of the many ingredients which led to a bitter and prolonged conflict.

THE SCHOOL

In a sense the hero, or villain, of this piece is the school itself. For

Dartington symbolizes for many people an important stream of educational radicalism, while, for people associated with it, it represents an alternative way of life, sheltering them from the perversities of modern society. This emotional linkage between educational liberalism and the bohemian intellectual has a long heritage, and this needs to be understood if the depth of reaction to my findings is to be appreciated.

Following the trauma of World War I, a particularly radical group of educationists founded schools. This group of radical experimenters accepted a Freudian interpretation of repression in early childhood leading to frustration and aggression in later life; a "free" upbringing, they avowed, would produce a new sort of person — the "self-regulated" individual — who would abjure hatred, prejudice, and wars and who would open the way for a more rational, benign, and tolerant society. In contrast to the public school, there was to be no uniform, no corporal punishment, no religious instruction, no compulsory sport, and no prefects. But there would be freedom to attend lessons, pupil participation in self-government, and opportunities for artistic and creative expression. However, because of their upper-class position, and because of their anti-urban values, these experimenters turned to the form of education for their social stratum, namely the private boarding school in the country. Yet their ideology was strongly anti-institutional and anti-authoritarian, and they fervently believed that they were providing a rich, but passive, environment where the self-willing individual would have the maximum freedom to grow and develop naturally without interference and without distortion.

Dartington Hall School opened in September 1926 with ten pupils. The early days were flexible, experimental, and apparently idyllic. Children generally loved Dartington. After a couple of years, the charismatic figure of Bill Curry was appointed headmaster and he remained its figurehead for some twenty-five years. Clearly, he was forceful and magnetic in building up the school in the 1930s; but, equally clearly, he was dispirited and disillusioned by World War II. Slowly his grip on the school slackened, and by the 1950s he was a despairing figure with the declining affairs of the school threatening an institutional collapse. His painful "resignation" on grounds of ill-health represents a traumatic watershed which few people at Dartington can face objectively. The Trustees appointed a married couple as joint-heads, Hu and Lois Child, and they, in endeavoring to put the school back on its feet again, elicited hostility from both the remaining Curry era pupils and the Curry era former pupils. After ten years of moderate success in fairly conventional terms, the Childs retired and made way for Royston Lambert, who reformed just about everything.

Initial Involvement with the Dartington Project

In 1965 I took an MA in sociology at the University of Essex. For some course work I was supervised by Royston Lambert at Cambridge. He was then director of the King's College Research Unit into Boarding Education, and helped me gain access to three traditional boarding schools for my master's thesis. In 1966 Lambert began a number of projects for the Public Schools Commission (promoted by the Labour government to explore possible integration between state and private education), and he offered me a one-year research assistantship to commence a doctoral project. This was to be on boarding education but there was no settled subject. Gradually I began to feel that observations would be socially more relaxed in progressive schools than in public schools. Ironically, then, I turned to progressive education partly because I thought I would feel more at home socially with progressives. But the prime reason was money; as an assistant on a year's contract, I was constantly on the lookout for funds to continue my research.

During my first year at Cambridge, Lambert was asked by the Elmgrant Trust of Dartington to find someone to carry out a follow-up study of former pupils of Dartington Hall School. The Trust was interested in sponsoring research at this stage because they were envisaging new developments in the school. The Childs were approaching retirement, while the Public Schools Commission which had just been constituted represented a certain threat to private schools. Presumably, the Trustees felt that research might shed light on how the school might be changed. But a considerable impetus for research came simply from a long-standing desire to find out exactly what had happened to their old boys and girls. Following an exploratory visit to the school with Lambert in May 1967 and a brief meeting with Leonard Elmhirst (chairman of the Elmgrant Trust at Dartington which was financing the research), the research commenced officially in September of that year.

There was no prior indication whatsoever from the Trustees of how they wanted the research to be carried out, except that they had accepted the skimpy research outline that I submitted to them. While Lambert was my academic adviser and the overseer of the project for the Trust, I was solely responsible for the execution of the research. I proposed to study three cohorts of Old Dartingtonians — from those who had left school in the late 1930s, the early 1950s, and the early 1960s — and also to observe the functioning of the contemporary school. But on starting the pilot interviews in the autumn of 1967, the first problems were encountered.

The major difficulty was that the school did not maintain a comprehensive up-to-date list of names and addresses for former pupils. Consequently, neither the school nor a former pupil society had systematically kept in touch with *alumni* as is common in public schools. In addition, the Childs first prevaricated about allowing me access to the school to use files to trace former pupils and then finally refused to let me in. This left me in the strange position, which was to last for some eighteen months, during which I was being paid by the Elmgrant Trust to study their school but was being denied access to that school by their employees. In fact, my proposed observational fieldwork in the school never did materialize.

This meant relying initially on the files of a woman who had organized the informal old pupil network for some years. Her files were by no means comprehensive and contained only a name and address. I decided, therefore, that a brief screening questionnaire should be sent to every former pupil simply to get sufficient information from which to draw a random sample of the population. Later, advertisements asking former pupils to contact the researcher were placed in a number of national newspapers and magazines (though with no great response). In effect, the interviews were carried out with people for whom the relevant information was available (date of birth, length of time at school, current address) and who were willing to be interviewed. They do not, therefore, constitute a statistically random sample either of the total Dartington population or even of the sub-sample at my disposal. This was to be of considerable significance later.

Altogether, sixty people from the two early cohorts were interviewed and this "sample" almost exhausted the number of eligible people who were available. At this state of interviewing, May–December 1968, the 1960s cohort went completely untouched as the details were still held in the school. Furthermore, because of fears that the sample might not be truly representative, and as the research was highly exploratory in nature, a fair number of "pilot" interviews with former pupils of interest were carried out. But throughout all this I was endeavoring to be methodologically sound on the assumption that this was essential for fulfilling the requirements of my dissertation. In the Research Unit we all read the standard literature on prisons, hospitals, schools, and communities, while observation was a key technique in the various projects. But on the survey side of the activities related to interviews and questionnaires, we were following orthodox methodological procedure, with a positivist sauce coating everything.

However, a number of "pilot" interviews were initially arranged with former pupils. Young was deeply involved in the research at first — going through the questionnaire with me and asking if he could accompany me on the early interviews. In fact, he only came to *one* interview, which was my very first. It also proved to be Young's last. This was with a rather neurotic young man in his early twenties who claimed to be an "evangelical Rocker." That meant that, clad in leather, he had "burn-ups" with "Rockers" (a British youth group of the 1960s associated with black leather, motorbikes, and mass fights with the rival "Mods") on his motorbike, while he also played the electric guitar in a religious pop group. His interview, in brief, turned out to be an exposé of the criminalesque subculture which can develop in progressive schools under the permissive umbrella (e.g., he had taken cars without permission, had sold art and craft products manufactured by children in the school to tourists, had got drunk, and so on). In particular, he had been constantly engaged in a war of wits with the Childs.

I think that first interview was an eye-opener for Young, from which he never recovered. He saw the progressive environment could be prostituted for the wrong ends by semi-delinquent adolescents and also how hostile some of the students were to the Childs. On the way back to London he expressed the view that material like that on the Childs could never be published. However, I completed the pilot interviews, revised the questionnaire, and endeavored to gain access to the school in order to use the files to trace former pupils. At this stage I wrote a short report on my pilot interviews and Lambert and I arranged a meeting with the Trustees to discuss the next phase of the research, the interviewing of the main sample. Of significance is the fact that, following Lambert's visit to Dartington the previous summer as part of his boarding schools' research, he had suggested some ways in which the school might develop and on the strength of that outline had been offered, and had accepted, the headship of the school for January 1969. The accession of Lambert made relationships with the Childs even more delicate.

We met in February 1968 in Young's house in Bethnal Green. Both Lambert and I were expecting the green light for the remainder of the research. But, to our surprise, Young asked me to drop the research altogether. If I wanted to study something else, then the grant would still be made available. Should I continue, then they felt that they could not put pressure on the Childs to grant me access to the school;

so the research on the contemporary school, and on the cohort that left under the Childs, would have to be shelved for the time being. I was profoundly depressed by this meeting, as I was midway through the second year of a PhD and felt that to stop now would leave me with nothing for my efforts while it was too late to commence a fresh project. After three months of depressive inactivity, I asked if I could continue the research on the understanding that the Childs' period should be shelved for the moment. The Trustees agreed, I continued interviewing and wrote a draft about my preliminary findings. Ash, the Trustee with responsibility for the school, replied that what I had written was very rewarding and well worth pursuing, but that there were serious doubts as to whether the completed study could ever be published.

I heard later that my paper, intended only for the Trustees, had been shown to one of the respondents, Su Isaacs, who immediately recognized her contribution and made a fuss about the possibility of identification in any forthcoming publication. Shades of things to come.

The Fieldwork Period

The bulk of the interviewing was carried out between October 1968 and July 1969 throughout Britain. In the autumn of 1968 I had registered as a research student at Essex University with Geoffrey Hawthorn as my supervisor. The Research Unit on Boarding Education moved to Dartington with Lambert and so I felt that I had lost my institutional base in Cambridge; I had also lost my supervisor. In October I intended to conduct a number of interviews in Devon and wrote to Ash requesting a convenient date to interview him. He replied, asking me to be as careful as possible in the locality in case the Childs found out I was active in the area, thereby raising "a hornets' nest."

In January 1969 the Childs retired and Lambert took over as headmaster. He invited me down to the school to use the manuscript sources in the school's files, and in March I spent two weeks working in the Records' Office. The personal files ("unsuitable for research," according to the Childs, because of their confidential nature) were in some disarray in a number of cardboard boxes, and for some time people, including the children, had had open access to them. I noticed that the Headmaster's Reports were incomplete. I also noticed that V. Bonham-Carter (1958), who had written the official story of the Dartington enterprise, had written a section on the school which had not been published. Bonham-Carter had mentioned the despair in Curry's final report to the Trustees. I asked the person in charge of the Records Office for this report. He replied that he did not know where it was but it certainly was not in the building. I then phoned Elmhirst to ask for the report, and, on his instructions, it was rather sheepishly produced. I heard later it was locked in the safe in the building. It was obvious from the report that Curry had given up hope and that the Trustess had little alternative but to ask him to leave. Yet I found it difficult to accept that the protectiveness which surrounded the document was justified.

During my visit to Dartington, I met Ash at his request. At this stage I was asking for more money to complete two groups of "control group" interviews with pupils of two other schools. Again, the very concept of "control group" reveals how tied I was to conventional methodological assumptions. I felt these were necessary for a respectably researched doctorate and, while I often despaired of ever completing a thesis (because of the methodological problems involved in having a biased sample), I persisted with the doctorate so that I should get something out of the research if publication was refused. In effect, Ash made the following conditions: that I drop completely the idea of interviewing a cohort from the Childs' era; that I agree not to discuss the Childs' era in my thesis; and that I sign a document giving Dartington exclusive rights over publication. I was reluctant to agree to the latter (which the Trustees had raised before but which was probably made urgent by my research on the files), but on Lambert's advice I agreed. At the same time, the Trustees wrote to Peter Townsend, chairman of the Department of Sociology at Essex, asking if they could have control over who could see the thesis when completed. But Townsend poured cold water on this.

I signed a document in April 1969, almost two years after I first got involved in the research, which stated that I could not publish anything arising from the research without the written consent of the chairman of the Trust. In addition, I would not allow anybody else to make use of my material (or of any thesis or report) without the written consent of the chairman, and that the material I had collected was to be deposited in the Records' Office at Dartington (where it would be available to me at all times but where written consent of the chairman would be required for anybody else wishing to make use of this).

Why did I sign? First, I needed money to finish the research. And second, as a research student, one is in a sort of limbo, cut off from institutional affiliations and estranged from the rest of the profession, and I had no unscrupulous colleagues to advise me as I do now. However, to preserve my chances of successfully completing my dissertation, I signed the document, which has remained to torment me ever since.

The Battle over Publication

In the autumn of 1969 I began the task of knocking my diffuse material into shape. A chapter on the history of the school grew beyond the needs of the thesis and I decided to write a separate paper, which I sent to the Trustees. To a certain extent, it revealed that the early years, before Curry's arrival and when the Elmhirsts' influence on the school was at its strongest, had been highly experimental. Elmhirst wrote that he hoped I would find a publisher and get it into print as soon as possible, while Ash also wrote in glowing terms. This point represents the high-spot of my relationships with the Trustees (they had progressed from "Dear Mr. Punch," "Dear Punch," and "Dear Maurice Punch," to "Dear Maurice"). That summer I wrote a short article hoping to get it published in the weekly social science magazine, New Society, and sent it to Dartington. Ash reacted unfavorably. I took account of his criticisms, recast the article, and sent it back to him. He replied that he was grateful for what I had done, that he did not object to publication of the revised article, but that he was passing it to Michael Young for a second opinion. Before I could dispatch the recast article, however, Michael Young phoned to say that the Trustees were against publication of the article or anything similar until my dissertation was completed. I concurred. By this stage I completed quite a few of the empirical chapters and duly sent them to Lambert. After a couple of months he sent them back unread, saying he did not have time to read them. In effect, he ceased to act in the overseer role as envisaged originally by the Trustees when he had moved from Cambridge and stopped supervising me.

In October 1970 I was offered a lectureship at Essex and preparation for teaching precluded a swift completion of the dissertation. Eventually, I finished it in early summer 1971 and it went off to the two external examiners who did not reach a decision for five months as one of them was abroad. Hawthorn, my supervisor, who was now at Cambridge University, wrote to Cambridge University Press recommending the dissertation for publication and they expressed their interest to me. I sent CUP a copy but warned them that Dartington had yet to give their permission. CUP sent the dissertation to a reader, who commented favorably while suggesting a number of revisions. Meanwhile, the

Trustees were considering the dissertation and my request for publication.

It is really at this stage that chronic mutual suspicion and mistrust made their entry and began to sour relationships. For instance, I would not disclose the publisher as I wanted an objective appraisal of my work and distrusted Dartington, whom I thought might try to influence the decision. I suppose I was hoping to present them with a "fait accompli" in terms of an offer of publication before they got a chance to slam the door in my face. The judgement of the Trustees was sent in July; as chairman, Elmhirst wrote that the Trustees could not allow the book to be published. He drew attention to the contract I had signed and warned me that I had actually broken that contract by passing the manuscript to a publisher without consent. This constituted "publication" in law. He requested that I withdraw the manuscript from the publisher. Despite this, he recorded their appreciation of my work and my enthusiasm and said that the report would be of permanent value to the Trustees and to the school. Later I was told that they had considered "slapping a writ" on me. Elmhirst proposed a meeting with the Trustees and Lambert in London once I had withdrawn the script from CUP. Elmhirst also wrote to Professor Townsend at Essex complaining that I had infringed the agreement and suggesting that I recover the script sent to the publishers immediately.

The Syndics of CUP were to meet on July 30 to decide on publication. The previous Monday Young phoned early in the evening to arrange a meeting for the coming Thursday. However, he made it plain that there would be no meeting unless I withdrew the script beforehand. I argued that an objective appraisal of the work's merits could not harm Dartington and that the publishers, whom I still refused to name, knew of the Trustees' veto so there was no question of their proceeding without permission. Michael Young was insistent and gave me a couple of hours to reconsider. When he phoned again I refused to withdraw the script. However, he now urged me to attend the meeting.

THE HIGHGATE SUMMIT

We met in London at Young's new house in Highgate (I was accompanied by Hawthorn). In the event, only Young and Ash were present for the Trustees. Ash said that the Trustees were anxious that a book be published but left most of the talking to Young. He launched on a long, lucid, and powerful methodological critique of the dissertation focusing particularly on the confidentiality of respondents and the lack of representativeness of the sample. But he began to make a number of suggestions as to how these points could be remedied. In brief, every effort would have to be made to guarantee anonymity; quotations from the school's files were confidential material based on correspondence with parents and could *under no circumstances* be quoted; and the unrepresentativeness of the sample meant that many of the conclusions were open to dispute. It was suggested that every respondent should read *the entire book* before consenting to quotations from their interviews. Eventually this demand was reduced to merely sending everyone a photocopy of the quote that I intended to use.

Basically, Hawthorn and I felt that we had been summoned to be told why the book could not be published whereas the Trustees now seemed willing to negotiate; indeed, Hawthorn said "then you do see a way clear to compromise?" and Young replied in the affirmative. We left the meeting convinced that the Trustees had agreed in principle to publication provided certain conditions were carried out, although they reserved the right to judge the revised work. I sent my version of the meeting to Leonard Elmhirst covering what I considered to be the agreement reached. Meanwhile, CUP wrote to say that the Syndics were strongly interested in a book based on my dissertation which should, however, incorporate their reader's suggestions.

I set about gaining permission to use individual quotes from respondents, who were sent a photocopy of their interviews. In my cover letter to respondents, I wrote:

> The Trustees have agreed to publication of the thesis and the Cambridge University Press has, at this stage, provisionally accepted it as the basis for a book on Progressive Education.

At this stage I was fairly confident that a compromise had been reached and that my revised version of the thesis would satisfy Dartington and CUP.

Very briefly, it might be best if I sketch in a few of my major conclusions, which were plainly critical of the school and which focused on three areas. First, it was argued that this type of "anti-institution," with its nebulous guidelines for action, is difficult to operationalize at a day-to-day level because so many of its concepts are imprecise and because they conflict with institutional imperatives for cohesion and continuity. Second, I felt that the ideal of "non-interference" by staff was often compromised by the staff's manipulation of the student society. But, in turn, the pupils could subvert the freedom offered to them with collective behavior, and by powerfully enforced group norms and sanctions, that were the antithesis of the school's most cherished values. And third, there was evidence to suggest that some of the former pupils found it difficult to adjust to the wider society, remained dependent on the school and networks of former pupils, were somehow undermotivated in terms of conventional achievements, and rather than taking an active part in changing the world, seemed to opt out into a peripheral, artistic subculture. In brief, I tried to give a sociological explanation of why there was a disparity between the school's aims — of institutionalizing freedom and creating a culture-free individual — and the actual performance as witnessed through interviews and documents.

THE BETHNAL GREEN SUMMIT

Early in the autumn term of 1971, Hawthorn phoned to say that he had had an angry telephone call from Young, who now wished to quash publication completely. He was so incensed by my letter to the respondents that he would not deal with me personally but was only, after much persuasion, prepared to meet Hawthorn in Cambridge. They met and talked for an evening during which Hawthorn tried to save the book. Eventually, a meeting was arranged which took place in early November. The week before the meeting I saw the examiners of the thesis, for my viva. While they rehearsed the now-familiar weaknesses of the research, overall they appeared to be enthusiastic and encouraging about it. However, they asked me to rework parts of it and resubmit it. While I was disappointed about not satisfying the examiners straight away, I was actually quite gratified that two sociologists had discussed it as a piece of serious research rather than as an embarrassing and threatening document.

Hawthorn and I met Young at the Institute of Community Studies, beneath a portrait of Leonard Elmhirst, and beneath the frowns of the blue-sheaved tones of the Institute's monographs (with their impeccable samples and irreproachable methodology). Young began by saying that I had made such a mess of things that it was only by Hawthorn's persuasion that he had been prevented from calling a halt to the whole business. In particular, he accused me of "perpetrating a deliberate lie" in my cover letter to respondents when I said that the Trustees had given permission for publication of the thesis. He said that an agreement to publish had not been reached at the Highgate meeting, and that I had *deliberately lied* to the respondents in order to get their agreement to use their interview material. I denied this strongly, saying that I was not the sort of person to employ those tactics. However, after Young had provoked me by referring to me several times as a liar (he may have intended to provoke me), I lost my temper and the meeting degenerated into something of a slanging match. I said, "you're talking a lot of bullshit," and he replied, "it's not bullshit." Then I said, "the Trustees are a load of shits," and Young said, "I'm glad you think the Trustees are a load of shits." And so it went on, with charge and countercharge, while Hawthorn sheltered in a corner. I only just managed to control my temper and fortunately did not erupt into physical violence — the defenestration of Bethnal Green would not only have brought me the unwelcome notoriety that one American sociologist attracted after socking a graduate student on the jaw, but would have led to an abrupt and disastrous termination of the project.

Eventually, Young stated that the only way out was for me to send a copy of the book to everyone I had interviewed so that they could have a *second* chance to see their quotes and to withdraw them. In addition, the respondents should have, as *a matter of professional ethics, the right to change what they had said during the interview.*

This was my first confrontation with professional ethics. I capitulated on all his demands but left feeling most upset and deeply depressed. In November 1971, Elmhirst wrote to confirm this agreement which contained twelve proposals along the now familiar lines. I was asked to sign the document. By now several members of the Sociology Department at Essex had read the thesis and were acquainted with the conditions that Dartington were trying to impose. On their advice I did not sign. It was departmental policy at Essex not to accept contracts which denied freedom to publish.

Around this time I went down to Dartington at Lambert's invitation to give a talk to the school staff. I sent two papers in advance as a basis for discussion. When I arrived, I discovered that some older members of staff were going to absent themselves to avoid an "emotionally disturbing experience," while several others produced a long critique of my papers, which opened:

> We are concerned that the pejorative tone of Mr. Punch's introduction may provoke an emotionally charged seminar in which reasonable discussion of his thesis will suffer. The purpose of this short paper is to ensure that certain important considerations are not submerged in a melee of recriminative details. In spite of its journalistic style, we are informed that this introduction is the outcome of serious sociological research and we feel that the first important step is to establish this research's credentials and credibility. Until this is done no further discussion is likely to be meaningful.

Ash, Elmhirst, staff, pupils, and some estate people were present, and the reception was somewhat cool and humorless although I had gone out of my way to be restrained. What impressed me was the inability of many people present to accept criticism about the school, and how emotionally defensive they were about my work.

Meanwhile I explored the possibility of a commercial publisher taking on the book (and taking on Dartington). I was informed, however, that the document I signed in April 1969 was legally watertight and that moral pressure was perhaps the best means of getting the Trustees to shift ground. Consequently, in early March 1972 I wrote to the Trustees asking them to look at my first revised version of the dissertation, i.e. the original "book" with the quotes vetted by respondents, which incorporated the critical insights of the by now numerous commentators who had read the original work. In particular, I objected to the idea of circulating a copy to everyone I had interviewed.

It took some time for all the Trustees to read this "revised version." Elmhirst responded first, with three pages of helpful notes on the text which ended by saying that he had enjoyed reading it and that when it was accepted and published he suspected that a lot of other people would be able to enjoy and appreciate the fruits of all my many months of labor. Young's comments were delayed by his work on the "College of the Air" in Mauritius but when they arrived they were, like Elmhirst's, apparently favorable (mentioning that his dissertation had been published as a book). Needless to say, I began to anticipate a similarly favorable response from the Trustees — Elmhirst was, after all, the chairman, and Young had been their main liaison and negotiator with me for almost two years.

THE COUP OF 1972

The Trustees met in July. Before that date, however, and unknown to me, there had been a bloodless "coup" among the Trustees which saw Elmhirst and his son removed and Elmhirst's son-in-law, Ash, installed as chairman (Michael Young was still away). The circumstances are obscure, but Elmhirst was squeezed out, and, now in his late seventies, he retired to California where he married Su Isaacs (a former pupil). The first inkling of their decision came from Lambert, who wrote to me that publication would damage the school's interests *at a very precarious moment in its evolution.*

The grounds of attack had changed from the methods of my research, which were now not irredeemable, to the unanswerable charge that publication would damage the reputation of the school at a delicate time. As an alternative, Lambert proposed that I be offered an "extended essay" in a book of essays on Dartington. It was merely left for Ash, writing a few days later, to reiterate this position. In the same week I heard from Essex that my resubmitted dissertation had been passed fit for academic consumption by its examiners.

THE LONG ROAD BACK

In October 1972 I wrote to Ash asking for details of the proposed symposium of essays on Dartington. After some months' delay he replied, but in the meantime I had written personally to Lambert, Young and Ash imploring them to reconsider their positions. This initiated a long, enervating, multi-sided correspondence in which I tried to wear down the Trustees. Their basic format for the proposed symposium was for essays on the school by Ash, Lambert, Young, and Millham and Bullock (the latter had worked with Lambert in Cambridge and had moved to Dartington with him). I was to be allowed two papers: one on the history of the school, and one on the "progressive adult" (this was the first time that Dartington acknowledged the existence of such an animal), together with a joint paper with Millham and Bullock on the progressive school. But to me the latter area was the kernel of my work, and I refused to cooperate along the suggested lines. I was holding out for three chapters, with one a sociological analysis of the school.

THE GREAT WESTERN HOTEL, PADDINGTON: A SHADY DEAL

Eventually, to discuss the proposed symposium a meeting was arranged in a seedy private room — where probably many an illicit liaison had been consummated — at the Great Western Hotel in Paddington Station in March 1973. The mood of the meeting was conciliatory. It was rapidly decided that I could have my full three chapters and that Lambert, Young, and Millham and Bullock should each write a chapter while Ash would act as editor and write an Introduction. My major concern was that agreement had been reached on my writing three chapters, and I left the meeting in an optimistic mood. I still had a lot to learn.

Several weeks later, I received a photocopy of Ash's letter to the literary agent which, to my surprise and contrary to our agreement, included the possibility of Su Isaacs (now Mrs Elmhirst) contributing a chapter. Ash replied to my protest that he had overlooked informing me owing to pressure of work. Because I was leaving for six months' sabbatical in Holland between July and December 1973, I completed my three chapters before departure and sent them to Ash. While in Holland I received the synopsis of Su Isaac's chapter, which proposed using *Curry's letters in the school's files*. This was in direct contradiction of Elmhirst's earlier letter to me that such material could never be published. But Ash assured me that he had no reservations about the confidentiality of this material in *her* hands.

THE SYMPOSIUM DEBACLE

When I returned to England in the New Year of 1974, I faced the thought of reopening negotiations with revulsion. This feeling was accentuated when I received a letter from Ash, which apologized for not sending me his draft Introduction, owing to an oversight, informed me that Lambert had categorically refused to write his chapter, hinted that Bullock and Millham's chapter was unacceptable to the Trustees, and mentioned that my suggestions for revision to my three chapters had been passed on to Young. Young would be writing his contribution *not as a sociologist*. By this stage, I had seen Isaac's contribution and Young's and was soon to receive Ash's "Introduction." Frankly, I was appalled by the low quality of the work that the Dartington people had produced. After years of carefully reworking my material, I exploded in the face of what I saw as their hastily thrown together drivel. I filled my pen with spleen and replied to Ash.

But at least Ash conceded the possibility that I might be allowed to publish a book of my own. To confirm this I phoned him and, in direct communication, he sounded weary and conciliatory. He conceded that I had behaved responsibly, that he had no objections to my publishing the three chapters, and that I could proceed to look for a publisher. This appeared to be a break-through, except that my three chapters had been written for a symposium and could hardly be expected to stand on their own. I pressed Ash to ask if I might use more of my original material and he replied in a qualified affirmative. I therefore dusted the copy of my "revised version" of 1971 and sent it, with apologies for the three-year delay, back to CUP. Their new reader replied enthusiastically in September but recommended some minor revisions!

THE BJS BURSTS ON THE SCENE

About the same time, an article on Dartington by me appeared in the *British Journal of Sociology* (Punch 1974). Technically, this piece was in contravention of my agreement with Dartington. But at Essex

I felt caught between the senior staff's "publish or perish" policy and Dartington's "publish and perish" ultimatum. I chose the former, and hoped that the academic format in a respectable journal might not cause too many shock-waves around Devon. But there is no doubt that this could be seen as a deliberate evasion of my contractual obligations. At Essex I had been told that my dissertation was not enough to obtain tenure and that I had to publish in an established journal. Once more, I was in a situation where my attempts to establish myself academically were being threatened by the long drawn-out machinations with Dartington. In trying to slip around the contract with Dartington by publishing an article without permission, I was being devious and, doubtless to them, provocative.

In January 1975 I returned to Holland to live permanently and in the spring began the revisions which the CUP reader had requested. One problem with successive revisions is that you become so filled with loathing for the typescript that it becomes almost impossible to approach it rationally and to see what needs correction. Your first reaction on looking at it is to vomit. I had now worked on two versions of the thesis, two versions of the book, and also on the three chapters for the symposium.

Halfway through the latest revisions, I opened a large envelope which had been lying around for some months. It had been forwarded from Essex and, judging by the envelope, I thought it contained a rejected article from the United States. It did. But the secretary at Essex had opened it, slipped a few letters for me in the envelope, and then resealed it. Amid the chaos of moving abroad and living in temporary accommodation, I turned belatedly to what I thought was yet another rejected article (you soon get used to it) when out tumbled a number of letters including one from Ash. Having read the *BJS* article, he was breathing fire and made threatening noises about my book. Had I opened the letter when it arrived I would never have bothered to begin the final revisions. Providentially, I had not opened it. Now I apologized to Ash and explained my predicament and, fortunately, he chose to accept my grovelling excuses. In June I finished revising the typescript, seemingly for the forty-second time, and posted it to Ash and to CUP. Eventually, in November 1975 Ash finally agreed to publication providing he and Young could write an Introduction.

I had also been asked by Bell and Newby, two former colleagues, to contribute a chapter on my Dartington saga to their proposed symposium on *Doing Sociological Research*. When I showed the draft of this to CUP I was advised not to publish it as it might jeopardize the future of the book and so I withdrew it. Bell launched a haughty missive in which he scolded my cowardly, irresponsible undermining of his joint enterprise (saying, among other things, "only don't expect anyone to take your signature on a contract seriously again. As far as I am concerned, you are both *legally and morally* obliged to produce a piece for us," my emphasis). It's those darned professional ethics again! I recast the article and made it less offensive and more analytical. It was rather ironical, then, when, on gaining legal advice, the article had to be withdrawn from the symposium. Bell and Newby commented on this cryptically in a guarded epilogue lamenting the British libel laws, and hinted that at one stage they had contemplated publication with a number of pages left blank as in a censored "Rhodesia Herald." They dared not even mention me and Dartington.

PUBLICATION: OR NOT QUITE?

Publication of my book was now set for early autumn 1976, and I nervously awaited its appearance. I received a letter from CUP in September saying that stock had arrived and congratulating me on the forthcoming publication in October. I was then shattered to hear, just a couple of weeks before publication, that CUP was not happy with the quality of the finished product which, principally because of faulty copyediting, contained too many errors. Rather than risk a poor-quality article, CUP decided to pulp the book and to reset it completely. Have you ever been pulped?

Shortly afterwards CUP received a letter which really did give me a heart tremor. A former pupil of Dartington had written a paper on Dartington when she was a student. She had let me see this and invited me to quote from it. When, however, I sent her a copy of my dissertation to read in 1973, she refused cooperation and asked for her material to be deleted. Having seen the advance publicity for the book, she was now pursuing CUP to ensure that the guarantee had been carried out. Unfortunately, it had not. I can only confess to having, inexcusably, left two quotes from her material in the text. Now I was petrified that this might be the last straw, and that Dartington would see my perfidy as irrefutable evidence of my inherent untrustworthiness. I pictured myself being drummed ignominiously out of the academic profession by the Ethics Committee of the BSA. If the worst came to the worst, and publication was quashed, then I was prepared to immolate myself on a burning raft, stacked with kerosene-soaked copies of my book, which was to drift down the River Dart past Dartington Hall.

Fortuitously, the postponement of publication enabled me to make last-minute revisions, and the offending quotes were expunged. The two quotes concerned were from responses to questions posed by the woman concerned in writing her term paper. It turned out that one was from Jennifer Platt, a sociologist, who willingly gave permission to use it (and who, ironically, had published a book criticizing the Institute of Community Studies' research methods: Platt 1971). To be on the safe side, however, the second quote was expunged as it came from a letter to the writer of the paper even though the woman concerned had given me written permission to use it. At this stage CUP insisted on playing safe in case the writer of the paper kicked up a fuss and delayed production further. Caution was required as my *BJS* article had been picked up by the media and had already elicited angry comments in *The Guardian* newspaper from Dartingtonians.

A week prior to publication, a reporter from the *Sunday Times*, who had got wind of the controversy behind the book (not through any effort on my part), phoned me and I told him precisely my viewpoint. Under the headline, "Dartington Study Backfires," the saga was aired publicly with a photograph of a couple of extracts from the dissertation marked "Deleted." The reporter had been to the University of Essex Library and compared the dissertation to the much slimmer book in order to trace the cuts. He wrote, "An academic time-bomb in the form of a highly critical book is to explode under Dartington Hall progressive school next Thursday." Ash commented that Dartington was "conned" by me, that CUP was trying to add a flavor of sensationalism to its "fuddy-duddy" image, and that he had refused to allow a photo of the school on the dust-jacket. The work, he added, would play straight into the hands of "the reactionaries of education" (*Sunday Times*, April 24, 1977). The book was suitably launched in April 1977 amid controversy and mutual recriminations (all of which guaranteed excellent pre-publicity for the work). It contained an hostile introduction by Young and Ash which predictably rejected all its findings. But the book was out!

Conclusions

Here I have endeavored to exorcise the Dartington debacle in a manner that sheds light on the personal, political, and moral dilemmas that can arise in research. The tedious, and for me loathesome, details are essential to appreciate the intricacies of the whole affair. I can only hope that recounting this saga renders it sociologically and methodologically valuable. The key issues raised — on confidentiality, sponsorship, identification, the freedom to publish, and the nature of professional standards — will be examined in the concluding chapter. In essence, the case reveals that, for participants in a conflict about research, ethics may be something of a luxury. For, in practice, personal and professional interests clash and intermingle in confused ways which make nice ethical distinctions difficult to make. An institution defending its reputation, and an academic fighting for his career, can engage in behavior that is desperate, emotional, and unscrupulous. Professional standards may disappear out the window, especially if the researcher finds ethical norms being used *against* him by members of his own profession.

4. CONCLUSION: MUDDY BOOTS AND GRUBBY HANDS

Some say Strodtbeck snooped, Burt fudged, and Humphreys should have snitched. Milgram shocked, Wiggins and Schoeck suffered, and Bersheid and Walters were shamed. Alpert and Leary tripped out, Josephson and others were kicked out, whereas Rainwater and Pittman were put out. James, as well as Kershaw and Small, were subpoenaed, and Nejelski and Lerman warn that more of us will be. And then there was Camelot. (References in original: Nom de Plume and Nilson 1979, p. 155)

Realities of the Field: Trust, Deceit, and Dissimulation

This book examines the relatively unexplored elements of the politics and the ethics of fieldwork. Taking a largely sociological and anthropological stance, and focusing mainly but not exclusively on observational studies, I have highlighted the issues particularly in terms of the *personal experiences* of the researcher, and his/her responsibility to the researched. For a number of reasons, academics do not always come clean on dilemmas faced in these two areas. We are then left either with bowdlerized accounts of the fieldwork experience or with reflection on issues related more to the institutionalized processing of projects than the moral dynamics of research. In contrast, I endeavor to take a forthright, pragmatic approach to areas frequently clouded over and neglected. I have set out to tackle ethical and political dilemmas in fieldwork in a practical, commonsense way that alerts students to the predicaments and pitfalls as well as pointing to guidelines for behavior and morals in the field. My view rejects both codes and "conflict-methodology" and argues for the moral force of academic convention as the most appropriate form of control for the conduct of observational and other research. Methodological preoccupations and predilections in social science mean that we are systematically denied information on crucial facets of the research process; this work helps to fill that gap by modestly attempting to eradicate a lacuna in the literature on qualitative methods.

The position that I take can be summarized as follows. Fieldwork takes us into a potentially vast range of social settings which can lead to unpredictable consequences for researcher and researched. The ethical factors associated with the control and regulation of social scientific research are accentuated in participant observation because the fieldworker often has to be interactionally "deceitful" in order to survive and succeed. Ethical codes fail to solve the situational ethics of the field and threaten to restrict considerably a great deal of research. The ethics of deliberate covert research is much more problematic, and I question seriously its validity. At the same time, in personal battles, as in my own with Dartington, codes and standards may seem irrelevant to the private struggle while they can be evoked to muzzle unappealing findings. Finally, I argue that openness, debate, individual responsibility, and professional accountability on the conduct of research are more likely to spell out a sensible and healthy approach to the moral dilemmas in fieldwork than regulation.

My position is based on reflection and analysis on my own research experience and of the standard literature. And here I wish to conclude in this chapter with attention being paid to the political, the personal and ethical features of research, for they are often intertwined in complex and confusing ways.

For instance, it is possible to conceive crudely of three models of fieldwork. First, there is the hypothetical "problemless" project where, say, a graduate student gains access to a fishing community, shares the men's hardships at sea, is accepted and rewarded with insights and data, and departs to write a description of that culture which the men accept (if they read it) as an adequate reflection of their life-style. There is no high drama, no trauma, and no hassles (rather like the classical ethnographers who could be sure that the Ashanti and Nuer would not be scouring the anthropology journals with their lawyers for negative references to tribal life). Second, there is the "knotty" assignment, say Spencer's (1973) study of West Point, where the institution erects barriers against prying outsiders, forcing the researcher to outwit the institutional obstacle course to gain entry and to penetrate the minefield of social defenses to reach the inner reality of a military academy. Access has to be negotiated, "secondary" access proves continually problematic, the research bargain is complex and not fully specified, and there may be disputes about publication in the interests of preserving the institution's reputation. The fieldworker may experience moral dilemmas, face feelings of betrayal, and be subjected to hostility on publication. The researched may privately acknowledge the accuracy of the analysis but find the time not ripe for publication, while in a factionalized setting (say, in a factory dispute between workers and management) the lower orders may feel "you're right but it doesn't do any good and only stirs up trouble for us in the end." Many studies of corporations, public agencies, and closed social groups that commence with the best intentions lead to dilemmas of role-playing in the field and of harm and identification on departure.

And, third, there is "ripping and running" ethnography, where the researcher deliberately employs concealment, say to the extent of posing as a full member of a religious sect, and then exits to acrimonious accusations of spying, lying, and betrayal while law suits and manipulation of publications sour the completion of the project. The researched may feel that they have been "ripped off," and the researcher may be dubbed a "wolf in sheep's clothing." The dividing line between two and three is difficult to draw in practice, but the legitimacy of the motives and methods is clearer for me in the former than in the latter.

The difficulty resides in the participant–observer's role, which is that of "part spy, part voyeur, part fan and part member" (Van Maanen 1978, p. 346). It is ironic, and even amusing, that academics end up in the same moral predicament as spies and other undercover investigators and even employ the same imagery of muddy boots (Fielding 1982, p. 96) and grubby hands (Marx 1980, p. 27). Many participant–observers cannot escape the realization that deceit and dissemblance are part of the research role and may not feel ethically comfortable with that insight. Lies, deceit, concealment, and bending the truth are mentioned in many reports of fieldwork (Freilich 1977); indeed, Berreman (1964, p. 18) states that "participant observation, as a form of social interaction, always involves impression management. Therefore, as a research technique, it inevitably entails some secrecy and some dissimulation." Where the gung-ho ethnographer is determined to penetrate social defenses, then he or she has to break down initial distrust in order to build a trustworthy identity (Hunt 1984).

If a latent aim of fieldwork is to create trust in the researcher, then what is the aim of that trust? And does not the relationship involve a double betrayal: first by them of you but then by you of them? In short, I believe that often in fieldwork the subjects are conning you until you can gain their trust and then, once you have their confidence, you begin conning them (Fielding 1982, p. 88). That element of interactional deceit may be inevitable but painful and even distressful for all parties. A fundamental canon for the fieldworker, however, is that he does not deceive himself. Morals in research are too important to be left to moralists, and, having misquoted Becker, I shall compound the blasphemy by misquoting Mills — ideally, every fieldworker should be his or her own moralist.

We have to acknowledge that the classics of the field reveal personal and moral dilemmas related to access, resistance to the researcher, involvement in deviant practices, factionalism, and deep feelings of obligation to the researched. Some researchers speak of fieldwork as personally transformative, leading to engagement and moral commitment (Wax 1971, p. 41) and to a close identification with the people studied (Becker 1970, p. 124). The frustration, fatigue, despondency, and ethical qualms that researchers experience are related partly to the fact that the semi-concious tactics of the field — eavesdropping, fudging over one's purpose, simulating friendship, surreptitiously reading documents, etc. — make for good data but bad consciences. You should not be exploiting your "friends." Any academic in his right mind would agree that research should display respect for persons and should not bring them harm, but fieldwork may inadvertently and unpredictably lead to the opposite. The ethnographic paradigm itself, in demanding a full, authentic, and colorful description of a culture, actually aids in making individuals and groups easy to recognize. After all, the road to "Urban Life" is paved with good intentions.

If we cannot be paragons in the field, then at least we can come clean in our publications and in analyses of the research process. Researchers may like to pose as moral entrepreneurs, in terms of exposing abuses in institutions and in terms of their paradigmatic purity, but the actual initiation and conduct of research are often related to "politics" that are mundane, personal, practical, and scarcely moral. Research in the context of funding, gatekeepers, "rabbis," fads and fashions, and careers is related to status, resources, negotiations, and enforced changes in research design (Platt 1976). Disagreement, confusions, misunderstandings, and project fragmentation are common to the research enterprise, and teamwork can lead to fundamental disputes (on workloads, division of academic labour, ownership of data, and publication) that materially affect the outcomes.

To illuminate the politics and ethics of fieldwork, academics are required to make explicit those hidden issues that are often glossed over. A longitudinal view from planning to publication (Manning and

Redlinger 1979) should anchor dilemmas within the "political economy" of rewards for research in universities and within the changing structure of resources, power, authority, time allocation, career lines, and funding agencies. There may be considerable cross-national differences here in terms of access, legal restraint (such as the libel laws in Britain), and employment for academics (with the majority of sociologists in the Netherlands employed by the government, which is the reverse of the position in the United States). Some of the constraints on academics in government are usefully explored by Nom de Plume and Nilson (1979), who describe the disparate multiple publics that can be involved in the complex negotiation of research. It is paradoxical that ethnographers can often subtly and colorfully explore the social construction of reality in a certain group but then go on to write of their research methods as if they were one-dimensional and unproblematic. Exploring these areas is essential to building up an analytical body of knowledge on the crucial area of morals and politics in fieldwork and other forms of qualitative research.

Research Obligations: Sponsorship, Confidentiality, and the Freedom to Publish

> Should we become a little, insulated, isolated bunch of folk using our means as an artificial barrier against the buffets of a highly critical, realistic, and competitive outside world? (Leonard Elmhirst 1937, p. 9)

In turning to the Dartington affair, I fervently hope that my personal academic nightmare should serve as a warning to all young researchers. *Never* sign away your rights to publication, however benign the sponsor may appear. After all, Dartington is renowned as a liberal institution, which is identified with research and which would be totally opposed to censorship in the arts. But when confronted with a sustained critique of their value-system, they reacted with irrational intensity and with a persistent attempt to suppress my work. In this light, the torturous battle between an obdurate institution and an obstinate individual can have more general lessons for the conduct and control of academic research. Most sponsors, I would suggest, may find it painful to have their protective myths pierced. This should be borne in mind by inexperienced researchers who might learn the subtle art of not treading too irreverently, and too unnecessarily, on institutional corns. Furthermore, research students might learn that the research process from original aim to successful publication is not always a harmonious progression but can be beset with fieldwork difficulties and with struggles to have the findings accepted.

Academics, for example, espouse the freedom to publish as one of the most fundamental rights of their profession. Sponsors, on the other hand, may feel that they have the right to control dissemination of the findings. Having paid the piper, they want copyright on the tune. Conflict on this may not crystallize until a very late stage in the research, when the sponsors begin to see themselves as an academic perceives them. The ensuing recriminations may be bitter. One way to avoid this is to keep the sponsor constantly informed of reports and plans for publication. But signing away one's rights to publications seems to me to be fatal. The most that an academic should concede is the right of the sponsor to be consulted prior to publication.

In my case I was a research student, reliant on Dartington for funds, and engaged on my first project. In Britain postgraduate students, in contrast to the situation in the United States, do not normally carry out structured course work, have little contact with their peers, and are often loosely connected with their university. They are generally in a weak institutional situation, facing temporary contracts and uncertain futures, and being highly dependent on supervisors and "rabbis" in the department. This structural weakness, taken with my low resources, meant that I could not contemplate legal action. In Britain it is often said that the courts are for the rich or the stupid, and I felt that Dartington was both. They had implicitly threatened legal action while lawyers for the Bell and Newby symposium advised that the position was "hopeless" because my material could be construed to be defamatory even if it was not intended to be so. While an appearance in the High Court might have appealed to my romanticism, the outcome could have crippled me financially.

One thing working in my favor, however, was the status of my publisher. I am sure that almost no final compromise could have been reached without the cool acumen and experienced negotiating skill of the "fuddy-duddies" at CUP (Patricia Williams and Elizabeth Whetton). A commercial publisher would almost certainly not have invested time and energy in combating Dartington on my behalf, given that Dartington was scarcely a subject that would stimulate sales of thousands of copies and lead to serial, TV, and film rights. Yet CUP threw its weight and reputation into the struggle and, seeing it as an issue of principle, resiliently countered Dartington and consistently restrained me with good advice.

I can imagine that Dartington viewed me as devious, untrustworthy, and unscrupulous. From my point of view, that is exactly how I saw them. When embroiled in a struggle riddled with mistrust, and with the accumulating misunderstandings that feed on that mistrust, it is difficult to think in terms of morals and ethics. Was I acting in good faith and Dartington in bad faith? Now that I had got someone really angry, where was Becker to tell me which side I should be on?

I have a strong feeling now that Dartington was almost an impossible institution to deal with. Should I have been more willing to compromise? I do not have a lot of patience and was perhaps unnecessarily abrasive in some of my letters (while maliciously enjoying tweaking their tails). But, on the other hand, there was Dartington's unscrupulous behavior in pushing Su Isaacs into the symposium deal without my knowledge and in allowing her to publish parents' letters which were denied to me.

In effect, I now consider that until 1973 I thought I was dealing with people with legitimate and responsible claims. From then on I lost patience and saw them as manipulative and as lacking scruples. There can also be no doubt that I am glad I held out for a monograph with CUP rather than publishing in a dreary volume of lacklustre Dartington contributions. Yet I cannot pretend that my motives were concerned solely with the pure pursuit of knowledge, in that I was determined to see my work in print almost regardless of Dartington.

At times, the research itself became insignificant besides the tenacious struggle not to let them win. There seemed no alternative but to chip away at their armor with a sustained, abrasive, but highly enervating, correspondence. And all the time, I was seeking ways to wriggle out from under my contractual obligations. By sending the manuscript to CUP, I was breaking the contract which I also deliberately circumvented in submitting an article to the *BJS*. It is clear that I was determined to complete my dissertation and get it published and, feeling that these were essential to academic advancement, I tried to evade Dartington's legal tentacles. Having the research registered as a dissertation proved my salvation; otherwise Dartington would probably have treated my report as a private document for their own use.

Out of this I might emerge as a slippery opportunist. Two aspects of the affair help to reduce this negative interpretation. First, I am convinced that it was basically impossible to deal with the constantly shifting constellations of Dartington opinion on the issue. Perhaps I prolonged the affair by relying on correspondence rather than on negotiation, but I half-consciously perceived that I was weak in face-to-face situations (while I felt intellectually intimidated by Young). But with Dartington, I was bounced between a founder who ostensibly espoused experiment, a new chairman who questioned the validity of the social sciences on philosophical grounds, a sociologist trustee espousing an impeccable formal model for research, and a sociologist headmaster guarding his own innovations — and, last but not least, what I construed to be the academic requirements of a doctorate.

Second, when the attack shifted to the grounds that publication would seriously damage the reputation of the school, then there was no defense. That is the researcher's Achilles heel, because he is tied to his research design and his data and they aid in molding his report, which may take several years to emerge. But in that time the sponsors may have changed their minds, or changed their personnel, and they may dictate that circumstances have changed and that this is not quite an appropriate moment to publish. It apparently never was an appropriate time at Dartington.

Yet one more sobering feature of the case is the fact that two sociologists played key roles. Lambert, who started as my academic adviser, was clearly caught in a dilemma when he took over the school and began to get apprehensive about how publication might affect his innovations. The role of Young is even less satisfactory. In some way he simply could not leave the research alone, but his interference was often needling and meddlesome. He led the attack in 1971, became subdued and conciliatory in 1972 when he was preoccupied in Mauritius, but became niggling again in 1973 when he started writing something on Dartington himself. Obviously, having two sociologists involved in a supervisory role in a project is no guarantee that they will sustain academic values and practice. One behaved just like a hostile trustee, and the other behaved like a defensive headmaster. They toed the party line rather than standing up for academic freedom. And then we talk about "professional" ethics and standards!

Indeed, one aspect that emerges most strongly from my research is the difficulty of studying an institution composed of literate, articulate, self-conscious people with the power, resources, and expertise to protect their reputation. The respondents too were not passive, but withdrew quotes and pursued the publisher to ensure that this had been done. Any mention of my work in an educational journal or newspaper led to someone grabbing his or her pen and sending off a robust rebuff of my research. As academics, desirous of completing research and getting it into print, we may resent this interference, but it is probably how most of us would behave if *we* were researched or interviewed.

Additionally, I cannot help now having a certain sympathy for

Dartington. People who sponsor research tend to feel that the knowledge gained is for their exclusive use and may resent its widespread publication. Dartington was the life-work of some of the people involved, and they invested many years and a great deal of money in the enterprise. My work attacked the most important feature of their lives.

I am prepared to concede that a more conciliatory, less abrasive, person than myself might have secured a swift and smooth solution. But such struggles are private ones, and you find yourself pretty much alone with little sustained support from colleagues. The more drastic solutions — such as appealing to the Council for Academic Freedom or writing an exposé article — all foundered on the fact that, throughout, there was always a slim hope of a compromise leading to publication (and also the fear that Dartington might take legal action). Unavoidably, the material recounted here tells something about me. A friend said to me, "I'd have reached a compromise in one afternoon," while an acquaintance surprised me, on hearing all the gory details, with the remark, "I'd really have enjoyed taking them on." I was able neither to compromise nor to enjoy it. All research depends to a greater or lesser exent on the character of the personalities involved, and in all sorts of ways individual abilities and weaknesses affect the outcome of our projects. Someone else may have handled the whole matter far more easily, and perhaps there was just a measure of incompatibility between my world and Dartington's that aggravated the suspicion and the lack of communication. Elmhirst even wondered if I had an underground wish to "bash" the school out of envy at never having had the chance to attend it!

I would like to think that this episode is an implicit confirmation of the deeply engrained academic principle that the results of research should be available for publication. The freedom to publish, like all freedoms, can never be absolute, but clearly the abdication of that freedom by a writer leaves him open to manipulation and censorship. Dartington were forced into a painful predicament by the findings of my research and even more so by the demand that they be made public. Their dilemma, and my embittering struggle with them, should serve both as a case-study of a liberal institution hoist on the petard of its own pretensions and as a cautionary tale for the academic community.

Indeed, my battle with Dartington impaled them painfully on their own value-system and perhaps revealed that such a liberal institution, ostensibly inviting critical research, is actually more deeply threatened by research — because it may expose debilitating gaps between precept and practice — than is a more conventional, established institution. To question the accepted myths of the progressives amounts, in their eyes, to a counter-ideology, and it becomes impossible to debate with them because they accept no neutrals — you are either for them or against them. This paranoia over evaluation arises partly from the fact that progressives wish to appear in the van of modernity and innovation while also feeling sensitive to their marginal position. This tends to lead to a schizoid attitude to research in that, in the search for legitimacy, positive findings are welcomed but negative data are dismissed with defensive rationalizations. There is even a fundamental, irrational hostility to research itself. It is ironic, for instance, that two institutions which also objected to the publication of research findings — the BBC and the Scientologists, the one an "establishment" organization and the other a religious sect (Burns 1977; Wallis 1976) — would both be anathema to the herbivorous progressives at Dartington.

It is perhaps ironic that I have gone from studying a British boarding school to researching the Amsterdam Police. The latter, ostensibly a reactionary arm of the repressive state apparatus, was not difficult about access, did not demand that I sign a contract, granted me access to sensitive areas of the institution (during a corruption scandal: Punch 1985), and has never interfered with my publications. Once, in a conversation with a radical criminologist, I was advised to infiltrate the police organization (capitalizing on the trust that I had built up), to gather secretly incriminating documents, and to publish these with the intention of causing maximum embarrassment to the police organization.

This gives some idea of the lack of consensus in the social scientific "profession" on legitimate research methods. In the Dartington saga I was continually asked to adhere to stringent norms regarding anonymity, confidentiality, use of files, and the approval of respondents for using quotes. No such uncomfortable requirements apply apparently to radical academics when researching institutions of the powerful who allegedly deserve to be exposed.

Does Dartington constitute one of those pernicious institutions? It is generally associated with the liberal, free-thinking sector of society and is not immediately associated with censorship, with banning books to the index, with forcing researchers to sign the Official Secrets Act, or with demanding the right to its "imprimatur" on all publications associated with it. Yet the one aspect my research accentuates above all is that the very antipathy to evaluation and hostility to publication (and fear of unfavorable publicity and disconfirming data) constitutes the most important piece of evidence that I collected in terms of revealing the "real" ideology and practice of Dartington. The consolation of a battle with sponsors, or of a struggle over the interpretation of the findings, is that the reaction to our data may provide the most telling piece of data of them all.

Conclusion: Common Sense and Responsibility

> The sociologist often experiences a certain guilt, a sense of having betrayed, a stench of disreputability about himself: these despite the covers, pseudonyms, and deletions with which he clothes his subjects. (Or, have I alone heard such "confessions" from fellow sociologists?) I would hold that it is just and fitting that he be made to squirm so, because, in having exploited his non-scientific self (either deliberately or unwittingly) for ends other than those immediately apprehended by his subjects, he has in some significant sense violated the collective conscience of the community, if not that of the profession. (Davis 1961, p. 365)

Social scientists engaged in, or responsible for, research on human subjects should be acutely aware of the moral dimension in their work. I am not very happy about this ethical dimension being translated into a code that restrains innocuous research and creates barriers where none are necessary. A code can be useful as a moral pathfinder sensitizing students, researchers, and supervisors to ethical elements in research prior, during, and after the project. But I agree with Holdaway (1980, p. 341) that "we should avoid the impression that research ethics are a clear-cut matter, based on a residual, all-embracing type of social scientists natural law."

Furthermore, codes tend to vagueness, do not provide specific operational guidelines (say, for the street ethnography of Weppner and his confreres), and lack an enforcement and sanctioning apparatus; and, while they may appear in the interests of the researched, they also symbolize "professional" status and respectability. They can also be a device to protect institutions against suits from the researched which is a not unimportant factor in a litigious society such as the United States.

The complexity and diffuseness of the issues involved and the large number of actors concerned (researcher, subjects, supervisors, the rest of the profession, people in the wider society, the media, etc.) argue against simple solutions or pat formulas. Research with human beings raises moral dilemmas that sometimes generate uncomfortable issues that can rebound on our professional standing. Presumably, few of us would wish to enjoy a professional self-image of social scientists as devious, deceitful, dishonest, and untrustworthy. Two additional reasons for questioning codes is that they may inadvertently end up protecting the powerful rather than the weak (Galliher 1982, p. 159). Also, the "paradox of policing" may lead to the consequence "that any means to insure conformity by enforcement of rules and regulations gives rise to their evasion" (Reiss 1979, p. 62).

But perhaps the strongest argument against any rigid imposition of standards and sanctions is that there is simply no consensus on the key ethical questions raised by our research. There is no hard-and-fast way to calculate the costs and benefits of social scientific research. Indeed, the debate on this area reveals polar extremes that are irreconcilable. We are not, as a profession, in a position to concur unanimously on what is harm, what is public, and what is private; which institutions are "reprehensible"; and when does the end of knowledge justify the scientific means? ("Scruples about being honest or the reputation of sociology count for little beside the possible benefit of further knowledge": Homan and Bulmer 1982, p. 114). I believe that most fieldworkers have only the haziest conception of what the philosophical and ethical arguments are and merely wish to immerse themselves blindly in the setting. I would concur with Roth's (1962, p. 284) healthy skepticism that researchers are more likely to resolve moral problems by "analyzing the research process of the sociologist himself than by drawing up written codes of ethics which merely perpetuate current moral biases and restrict rather than aid further ethical development."

At that level, in the field, a measure of mutual deception and impression management may well develop that always borders on the edge of deception and untruth but is interactionally unavoidable and morally tolerable. To a greater or lesser extent, people are evasive and may lie (Van Maanen 1979, p. 539), and the researcher may feel that some degree of duplicity is required to penetrate fronts and conceal his real purpose; "this sounds insidious and even unethical or somewhat immoral, but everyone employs this technique to some degree in everyday life" (Reynolds 1982, p. 208).

It is a quite different matter if the researcher before entry consciously sets out to employ deception and deceit or to infiltrate covertly certain groups. That is skating on moral and scientific thin ice. And I am not at all sure that it is the academic's task to penetrate government and business in order to expose them; perhaps the run-of-the-mill fieldworker tends to amorality and even lacks moral and ideological zeal (Dingwall et al. 1980, p. 4). He feels that exposé research is best left to the investigative reporter. For investigative journalism is risky, time-consuming, hit-and-miss, requires special skills and even financial resources for informants, and is rarely presented in an academic format. Given that most academics desire scientific recognition, this is not usually the path to a dissertation or a chair (Doig 1984). We may dream of stumbling on something that will change the course of history — and if Woodward and Bernstein had been held to federal standards for the conduct of research, then Watergate might not have happened (Klockars 1979, p. 264) — but that is illusory if we seriously examine the sorts of subjects that ethnographers study (taxi-drivers, cocktail waitresses, embalmers, musicians, auctioneers, winos, and bums).

And, in a sense, the more "journalistic" social science becomes, the easier it is for its opponents to dismiss it as non-scientific. This leads to social science being seen as trivial in its results and dangerous in its techniques, making it "simultaneously impotent and threatening" (Reiss 1979, p. 93). Researchers "fish in troubled waters," while research on human subjects potentially reveals secrets, violates privacy, and destroys or harms reputations (Becker 1970, p. 108). It is scarcely surprising, then, that people who consider themselves powerful and important will endeavor to protect their reputations, their wealth, or their power. Powdermaker (1966), had problems of access in Hollywood; Argyris (Van Maanen 1978, p. 324) had to traipse around umpteen banks before getting his foot in the vault of one; and Wax (1971, p. 47) remarks that, if the researcher "tries to obtain membership in elite groups (such as physicians, big business executives, Orthodox Jews), he will soon 'observe' that most doors are firmly closed in his face." Indeed, Rock (1979, p. 261) states baldly that "no sociologist I know would himself agree to become a subject of observational research." My concern is that conflict methodology can spell the death of fieldwork, and that will be especially true of the very organizational areas it wishes to invade.

Where does that leave us? With no code, no consensus, and no conflict methodology, should we all enrol for factor analysis? My answer is that we should rely on *common sense* — a characteristic that some may not readily attribute to academics in general or social scientists in particular. Common sense, academic convention, and peer control through discussion are more likely to promote understanding of the issues and compliance with them.

Universities should take into account the ethical dimension of research (say, using current codes as a *guideline*); supervisors should alert students and researchers to the moral component of fieldwork; and academics should be highly sensitive to the consequences of their research for the subjects concerned. We should be conscious that observational studies can have a predatory character (Rock 1979, p. 201) and can invade sensitive areas. As a consequence, we should be aware of the moral and institutional force of academic convention in demanding that we do not lie, cheat, steal, or break promises to subjects. Often fieldwork means getting to like the researched and hoping they will get to like you. On that basis, it is reprehensible if we train students to purloin documents, betray confidences, and abjure the strong obligations surrounding friendship in our society. A healthy academic community concerns itself with responsibility to the researched, accountability to colleagues, and integrity in terms of responsible conduct between senior and junior staff (to avoid feudal exploitation).

If the researched are seen as "collaborators" in the research, rather then as "subjects," then we should behave towards them as we are expected to behave towards friends and acquaintances in our own daily lives. Abandoning the field without consideration for the consequences is a form of betrayal, and exposing the institution also exposes our previous "partners" who let us into their world on the implicit understanding of secrecy about their deviant and concealed antics. At the same time, this does allow us to recognize an interactional element of "cheating," not telling the whole truth, and impression management in order to build up relationships and to get at certain types of data. This is unavoidable, and is tolerable provided it is not consciously and cynically manipulated to the disadvantage of the researched.

In the last resort, I believe that much fieldwork is innocuous and unproblematic and that codes and regulations will only hamper it. I doubt too if many social scientists are happy about the sort of professional control and sanctions that may be appropriate in other occupations. There always will be a Humphreys seeing what he can get away with, and I do not see how we can stop him. And I am not sure I really want to.

Finally, I stand for common sense in relation to our research subjects and also for responsibility towards our discipline. There are worlds out there waiting to be explored. If we wish to be taken seriously, to conduct serious research, and to negotiate legitimate access to areas of power, then we cannot engage in "rip-off" ethnography (at least, not more than *once*). Doors will be closed, our discipline will be discredited, and we will have no one to study but the poor, the disadvantaged, and the marginal. In that light, conflict methodology is in danger of being exposed as a flatulent, and even fraudulent, rhetoric. It would ultimately serve to magnify our failure to study the powerful. That would leave us with the painful revelation that, behind the radical and threatening image, the social scientist is a sheep in sheep's clothing.

REFERENCES

Agar, M. 1973. *Ripping and Running: A Formal Ethnography of Urban Heroin Addicts.* New York and London: Seminar Press.
———. 1980. *The Professional Stranger.* New York: Academic Press.
American Sociologist 1978. Special issue on "Regulation of Research." 13.
Argyris, C. 1969. Diagnosing defences against the outsider, pp., 115–127 in G.J. McCall and J.L. Simmons (eds), *Issues in Participant Observation.* Reading, Mass.: Addison-Wesley.
Atkinson, M. 1977. Coroners and the categorisation of deaths as suicides: Changes in perspective as features of the research process, pp. 31–46 in C. Bell and H. Newby (eds), *Doing Sociological Research.* London: Allen & Unwin.
Baldamus, W. 1972. The role of discoveries in social science, pp. 276–302 in T. Shanin (ed.), *The Rules of the Game.* London: Tavistock.
Barber, B. 1976. The ethics of experimentation with human subjects. *Scientific American* 234 (2): 25–31.
Barnes, J.A. 1979. *Who Should Know What? Social Science, Privacy and Ethics.* Harmondsworth: Penguin.
Becker, H.S. 1963. *Outsiders.* New York: Free Press.
———. 1967. Whose side are we on? *Social Problems* 14: 239-247.
———. 1970. *Sociological Work.* London: Allen Lane.
Bell, C. 1977. Reflections in the Banbury restudy, pp. 47–66 in C. Bell and H. Newby (eds), *Doing Sociological Research.* London: Allen & Unwin.
——— and Newby, H. 1972. *Community Studies.* London: Allen & Unwin.
———. (eds) 1977. *Doing Sociological Research.* London: Allen & Unwin.
Berghe, P. van der 1968. Research in South Africa, pp. 183–197 in G. Sjöberg (ed.) *Ethics, Politics and Social Research.* Cambridge, Mass.: Schenkman.
Berreman, G.D. 1964. *Behind Many Masks: Ethnography and Impression Management in a Himalayan Village.* Ithaca, NY: Society for Applied Anthropology, Monograph No. 4.
Bogdan, R. 1972. *Participant Observation in Organizational Settings.* Syracuse, NY: Syracuse University Press.
Bok, S. 1978. *Lying.* New York: Pantheon.
Bonham-Carter, V. 1958. *Dartington Hall.* London: Phoenix House.
Boruch. R.F. and Cecil, J.S. 1983. *Solutions to Ethical and Legal Problems in Social Research.* New York: Academic Press.
Bottomore, T., Nowak, S. and Sokolowska M. (eds) 1980. *Sociology: The State of the Art.* Beverly Hills, Calif.: Sage.
Braithwaite, J. 1985. Corporate Crime Research. *Sociology* 19(1): 136-8.
Brandt, A.M. 1978. *Racism, Research and the Tuskegee Syphilis Study.* New York: Hastings Center Report 8.
Broad, W. and Wade, N. 1983. *Betrayers of the Truth: Fraud and Deceit in the Halls of Science.* New York: Simon and Schuster/Touchstone.
Bulmer, M. (ed.) 1982. *Social Research Ethics.* London: Macmillan.

Burgess, R.G. (ed.) 1982. *Field Research: A Sourcebook and Field Manual*. London: Allen & Unwin.

Burns, T. 1977. *The B.B.C.* London: Macmillan.

Cain, M. and Finch, J. 1980. The rehabilitation of data. Paper presented at BSA Annual Conference, University of Lancaster.

Caudill, W. 1958. *The Psychiatric Hospital as a Small Society*. Cambridge, Mass.: Harvard University Press.

Chatterton, M.R. 1978. From participant to observer. *Sociologische Gids* 25 (6): 502–516.

Clarke, M. 1975. Survival in the field: Implications of personal experience in field-work. *Theory and Society* 2 (1): 95–123.

Cohen, S. and Taylor, L. 1970. The experience of time in long-term imprisonment. *New Society* 31 December.

———. 1972. *Psychological Survival: The Experience of Long-Term Imprisonment*. Harmondsworth: Penguin.

———. 1977. Talking about prison blues, pp. 67–86 in C. Bell and H. Newby (eds), *Doing Sociological Research*. London: Allen & Unwin.

Dalton, M. 1959. *Men Who Manage*. New York: John Wiley.

———. 1964. Preconceptions and methods in men who manage, pp. 50–95 in P. Hammond (ed.), *Sociologists at Work*. New York: Basic Books.

Davis, F. 1961. Comment on "Initial Interactions of Newcomers in Alcoholics Anonymous." *Social Problems* 8: 364–365.

Denfield, D. (ed.) 1974. *Street-wise Criminology*. Cambridge, Mass.: Schenkman.

Denzin, N.K. 1970. *The Research Act*. Chicago: Aldine.

——— and Erikson, K. 1982. On the ethics of disguised observation: An exchange, pp. 142–151 in M. Bulmer (ed.), *Social Research Ethics*. London: Macmillan.

Diamond, S. 1964. Nigerian discovery: The politics of field-work, pp. 119–154 in A.J. Vidich, J. Bensman and M.R. Stein (eds), *Reflections on Community Studies*. New York: Harper & Row.

Diener, E. and Crandall, R. 1978. *Ethics in Social and Behavioral Research*. Chicago: University of Chicago Press.

Dingwall, R., Payne, C. and Payne, I. 1980. The development of ethnography in Britain. Oxford: Centre for Sociolegal Studies, mimeo.

Ditton, J. 1977. *Part-Time Crime*. London: Macmillan.

Doig, A. 1984. *Corruption and Misconduct in Contemporary British Politics*. Harmondsworth: Penguin.

Douglas, J.D. (ed.) 1970. *Observations of Deviance*. New York: Random House.

———. (ed.) 1976. *Investigative Social Research*. Beverly Hills, Calif.: Sage.

———. 1979. Living morality versus bureaucratic fiat, pp. 13–33 in C.B. Klockars and F.W. O'Connor (eds), *Deviance and Decency*. Beverly Hills, Calif.: Sage.

Downes, D. and Rock, P. 1982. *Understanding Deviance*. Oxford: Oxford University Press.

Elmhirst, L.K. 1937. *Faith and Works*. Totnes: Dartington Hall.

Emerson, R. (ed.) 1983. *Contemporary Field Research*. Boston: Little Brown.

Faris, R. 1967. *Chicago Sociology*. Chicago: Chicago University Press.

Festinger, L., Riecken, H.W. and Schachter, S. 1956. *When Prophecy Fails*. New York: Harper & Row.

Fielding, N. 1982. Observational research on the National Front, pp. 80–104 in M. Bulmer (ed.), *Social Research Ethics*. London: Macmillan.

Filstead, W.J. (ed.) 1972. *Qualitative Methodology*. Chicago: Rand McNally.

Florez, C.P. and Kelling, G.L. 1979. Issues in the use of observers in large-scale program evaluation: The hired hand and the lone wolf. Unpublished paper, Kennedy School of Government, Harvard University.

"Footnotes". 1982. Washington, DC: American Sociological Association, March.

"Footnotes". 1984. Washington, DC: American Sociological Association, October.

Freilich, M. (ed.) 1977. *Marginal Natives at Work*. New York: John Wiley.

Galliher, J.F. 1982. The protection of human subjects: A re-examination of the professional code of ethics, pp. 152–165 in M. Bulmer (ed.), *Social Research Ethics*. London: Macmillan.

Gans, H.J. 1962. *The Urban Villagers*. New York: Free Press.

———. 1967. *The Levittowners*. London: Allen Lane.

Goffman, E. 1959. *The Presentation of Self in Everyday Life*. Harmondsworth: Penguin.

———. 1961. *Encounters*. Harmondsworth: Penguin.

———. 1971. *Relations in Public*. Harmondsworth: Penguin.

———. 1972. *Interaction Ritual*. Harmondsworth: Penguin.

Golde, P. (ed.) 1970. *Women in the Field: Anthropological Experiences*. Chicago: Aldine.

Gray, B.H. 1979. The regulatory context of social research: The work of the National Commission for the Protection of Human Subjects, pp. 197–223 in C.B. Klockars and F.W. O'Connor (eds), *Deviance and Decency*. Beverly Hills, Calif.: Sage.

Hammersley, M. and Atkinson, P. 1983. *Ethnography: Principles in Practice*. London: Tavistock Press.

Hammond, P. (ed.) 1964. *Sociologists at Work*. New York: Basic Books.

Holdaway, S. 1980. *The Occupational Culture of Urban Policing: An Ethnographic Study*. Unpublished PhD, University of Sheffield.

———. 1982. "An inside job": A case study of covert research on the police, pp. 59–79 in M. Bulmer (ed.), *Social Research Ethics*. London: Macmillan.

———. 1983. *Inside the British Police*. London: Basil Blackwell.

Homan, R. and Bulmer, M. 1982. On the merits of covert methods: A dialogue, pp. 105–124 in M. Bulmer (ed.), *Social Research Ethics*. London: Macmillan.

Horowitz, I.L. 1970. Sociological snoopers and journalistic moralizers. *Transaction* 7: 4–8.

Humphreys, L. 1970. *Tearoom Trade: Impersonal Sex in Public Places*. Chicago: Aldine.

Hunt, J. 1984. The development of rapport through the negotiation of gender in field work among police. *Human Organization* 43 (4): 283–296.

Jarvie, I.C. 1969. The problem of ethical integrity in participant observation. *Current Anthropology* 10 (5): 505–508.

Johnson, J.M. 1975. *Doing Field Research*. New York: Free Press.

Junker, B.H. (ed.) 1960. *Field Work*. Chicago: University of Chicago Press.

Katz, J. 1972. *Experimentation with Human Beings*. New York: Russell Sage.

Kirkham, G.L. 1974. From professor to patrolman. *Journal of Police Science and Administration* 2 (2): 127–137.

Klein. L. 1976. *A Social Scientist in Industry*. London: Gower.

Klockars, C.B. 1979. Dirty hands and deviant subjects, pp. 261–282 in C.B. Klockars and F.W. O'Connors (eds), *Deviance and Decency*. Beverly Hills, Calif.: Sage.

——— and O'Connor, F.W. (eds) 1979. *Deviance and Decency: The Ethics of Research with Human Subjects*. Beverly Hills, Calif.: Sage.

La Pierre, R.T. 1934. Attitudes vs actions . *Social Forces* 13: 230–237.

Lazarsfeld, P.F. and Rosenberg, M. (eds) 1955. *The Language of Social Research*. Glencoe, Ill.: Free Press.

Liebow, E. 1967. *Tally's Corner*. Boston: Little Brown.

Lofland, J.F. 1971. *Analyzing Social Settings*. New York: Wadsworth.

———. 1976. *Doing Social Life*. New York: John Wiley.

——— and Lejeune, R.A. 1960. Initial interaction of newcomers in Alcoholics Anonymous. *Social Problems* 8: 102–111.

Lowry, R. 1972. Towards a sociology of secrecy and security systems. *Social Problems* 19: 68–77.

Lurie, A. 1967. *Imaginary Friends*. London: Heinemann.

McCall, G. and Simmons J.L. (eds) 1969. *Issues in Participant Observation*. Reading, Mass.: Addison Wesley.

Malinowski, B. 1967. *A Diary in the Strict Sense of the Term*. New York: Harcourt, Brace and World.

Manning, P.K. 1972. Observing the police, pp. 213–268 in J.D. Douglas (ed.), *Research on Deviance*. New York: Random House.

——— and Redlinger, L.J. 1979. The political economy of fieldwork ethics, pp. 125–148 in C.B. Klockars and F.W. O'Connor (eds), *Deviance and Decency*. Beverly Hills, Calif.: Sage.

——— and Van Maanen, J. (eds) 1978. *Policing: A View from the Street*. Santa Monica, Calif.: Goodyear.

Martin, S.E. 1980. *Breaking and Entering*. Berkeley, Calif.: University of California Press.

Marx, G. 1980. Notes on the discovery, collection and assessment of hidden and dirty data. Unpublished paper, delivered at SSSP Annual Meeting, New York.

Mead, M. 1961. The human study of human beings. *Science* 133: 163–165.

Milgram, S. 1963. Behavioral study of obedience. *Journal of Abnormal and Social Psychology* 67: 371–378.

———. 1974. *Obedience and Authority*. London: Tavistock Press.

Mills, C.W. 1959. *The Sociological Imagination*. New York: Oxford University Press.

Morgan, D.H.J. 1972. The British Association scandal: The effect of publicity on a sociological investigation. *Sociological Review* 20 (2): 185–206.

Newby, H. 1977. In the field: Reflections on the study of Suffolk farm workers, pp. 108–129 in C. Bell and H. Newby (eds), *Doing Sociological Research*. London: Allen & Unwin.

Nom de Plume and Nilson D.R. 1979. Politics of research ethics in a federal bureaucracy, pp. 151–173 in C.B. Klockars and F.W. O'Connor (eds.), *Deviance and Decency*. Beverly Hills, Calif.: Sage.

O'Connor, F.W. 1979. The ethical demands of the Belmont Report, pp. 225–258 in C.B. Klockars and F.W. O'Connor (eds), *Deviance and Deviancy*. Beverly Hills, Calif.: Sage.

Payne, G., Dingwall, R., Payne, I. and Carter, M.P. 1981. *Sociology and Social Research*. London: Routledge & Kegan Paul.

Platt, J. 1971. *Social Research in Bethnal Green*. London: Macmillan.

———. 1976. *The Realities of Social Research*. London: University of Sussex Press.

Poel, S. van der 1981. Wolf in Schaapsvacht. Paper presented at NSAV conference, Utrecht.

Polsky, N. 1971. *Hustlers, Beats and Others*. Harmondsworth: Penguin.

Powdermaker, H. 1966. *Stranger and Friend: The Way of an Anthropologist*. New York: W.W. Norton.

Punch, M. 1974. The sociology of the anti-institution. *British Journal of Sociology* 25 (3): 312–325.

———. 1977. *Progressive Retreat*. Cambridge: Cambridge University Press.

———. 1979. *Policing the Inner City*. London: Macmillan.

———. 1985. *Conduct Unbecoming: The Social Construction of Police Deviance and Control*. London: Tavistock Press.

Reiman, J.H. 1979. Research subjects, political subjects, and human subjects, pp. 35–37 in C.B. Klockars and F.W. O'Connor (eds), *Deviance and Decency*. Beverly Hills, Calif.: Sage.

Reiner, R. 1979. Assisting with enquiries: Problems of research on the police. Paper presented to British Sociological Association Conference, Warwick University.

Reisman, M. 1979. *Folded Lies*. New York: Free Press.

Reiss, A.J. Jr. 1966. The study of deviant behavior: Where the action is. *Ohio Valley Sociologist* 32: 60–66.

———. 1968. Stuff and nonsense about social surveys and observation, pp. 351–367 in H.S. Becker, B. Geer, D. Reisman and R.S. Weiss (eds), *Institutions and the Person*. Chicago: Aldine.

———. 1979. Governmental regulation of scientific enquiry: Some paradoxical consequences, pp. 61–95 in C.B. Klockars and F.W. O'Connor (eds), *Deviance and Decency*. Beverly Hills, Calif.: Sage.

Reynolds, P.D. 1979. *Ethical Dilemmas in Social Science Research*. San Francisco, Calif.: Jossey-Bass.

———. 1982. Moral judgements: Strategies for analysis with application to covert participant observation, pp. 185–216 in M. Bulmer (ed.), *Social Research Ethics*. London: Macmillan.

Riecken, H.W. 1969. The unidentified interviewer, pp. 39–44 in G.J. McCall and J.L. Simmons (eds), *Issues in Participant Observation*. Reading, Mass.: Addison-Wesley.

Riemer, J.W. 1979. *Hard Hats*. Beverly Hills, Calif.: Sage.

Roberts, H. 1981. *Doing Feminist Research*. London: Routledge & Kegan Paul.

Rock, P. 1979. *The Making of Symbolic Interactionism*. London: Macmillan.

Roth, J.A. 1962. Comments on "secret observation." *Social Problems* 9 (3): 283–284.

———. 1963. *Timetables*. New York: Bobbs-Merrill.

Rynkiewich, M.A. and Spradley, J. (eds) 1976. *Ethics and Anthropology: Dilemmas in Fieldwork*. New York: John Wiley.

Sagarin, E. and Moneymaker, J. 1979. The dilemma of researcher immunity, pp. 175–193 in C.B. Klockars and F.W. O'Connor (eds), *Deviance and Decency*. Beverly Hills, Calif: Sage.

Schaffir, W.B., Stebbins, R.A. and Tierowetz, A. (eds) 1980. *Fieldwork Experience*. London: St Martins Press.

Schatzman. L. and Strauss, A. 1973. *Field Research: Strategies for a Natural Sociology*. Englewood Cliffs, NJ: Prentice-Hall.

Schwartz, M. 1964. The mental hospital: The researched person in the disturbed ward, pp. 85–117 in A.J. Vidich, J. Bensman and M. Stein (eds), *Reflections on Community Studies*. New York: Harper & Row.

Schwartz, H. and Jacobs, J. 1979. *Qualitative Sociology*. New York: Free Press.

Shanin, T. (ed.) 1972. *The Rules of the Game*. London: Tavistock Press.

Sharrock, W. and Anderson, R. 1980. Ethnomethodology and British sociology: Some problems of incorporation. Paper presented at BSA Annual Conference, University of Lancaster.

Shils, E. 1982. Social enquiry and the autonomy of the individual, pp. 125–141 in M. Bulmer (ed.), *Social Research Ethics*. London: Macmillan.

Short, J.F. (ed.) 1980. *The State of Sociology*. Beverly Hills, Calif.: Sage.

Sjöberg, G. (ed.) 1968. *Ethics, Politics and Social Research*., Cambridge, Mass.: Schenkman.

Skidelsky, R. 1969. *English Progressive Schools*. Harmondsworth: Penguin.

Skolnick. J.H. 1975. *Justice Without Trial* (2nd edn). New York: John Wiley.

Smith-Bowen, E. 1964. Return to Laughter. New York: Random House.

Social Problems 1973. Special issue on "The Control of Social Research", 21: 1.

——. 1980. Special issue on "Ethical Problems of Field-Work." 27: 3.

Soloway, I. and Walters, J. 1977. Working the corner, pp. 159–178 in R.S. Weppner (ed.), *Street Ethnography*. Beverly Hills, Calif.: Sage.

Spencer. G. 1973. Methodological issues in the study of bureaucratic elites: A case of West Point. *Social Problems* 21 (1): 90–102.

Srinivas, M.N., Shah, A.M. and Ramaswamy, E.A. (eds) 1979. *The Fieldworker and the Field*. Delhi: Oxford University Press.

Sullivan, M.A., Queen, S.A. and Patrick, R.C. 1958. Participant observation as employed in the study of a military training program. *American Sociological Review* 23: 610–667.

Sunday Times 1977. Dartington Study Backfires, 24 April.

Thompson, H. 1967. *Hell's Angels*. Harmondsworth: Penguin.

Van Maanen, J. 1978. On watching the watchers, pp. 309–349 in P.K. Manning and J. Van Maanen (eds), *Policing: A View from the Street*. Santa Monica, Calif.: Goodyear.

Van Maanen, J. (ed.) 1979. Qualitative Methodoloy. Special issue. *Administrative Science Quarterly*. 24 (4): 519–680.

——. 1984. Tales of the field, forthcoming in D.H. Berg and K.K. Smith (eds) *The Clinical Demands of Research Methods*. Beverly Hills, Calif.: Sage.

——. 1985. Power and the bottle, draft paper, Cambridge, Mass.: MIT.

Vidich, A.J. and J. Bensman 1958, 1968. *Small Town in Mass Society*. Princeton, NJ.: Princeton University Press. (First published in 1958; revised edition 1968.)

Vidich, A.J., Bensman, J. and Stein, M.R. (eds) 1964. *Reflections on Community Studies*. New York: John Wiley.

Wallis, R. 1973. Religious sects and the fear of publicity, *New Society*, 24: 545–547.

——. 1976. *The Road to Total Freedom*. London: Heinemann.

——. 1977. The moral career of a research sociologist, pp. 149–169 in C. Bell and H. Newby (eds), *Doing Sociological Research*. London: Allen & Unwin.

Wallraff, G. 1979. *Beeld van Bild*. Amsterdam: Van Gennep.

Warwick, D.P. 1982. Tearoom trade: Means and ends in social research, pp. 38–58 in M. Bulmer (ed.) *Social Research Ethics*. London: Macmillan.

Watkins, J.W.N. 1963. Confession is good for ideas, *The Listener*, 69, 18 April: 667–668.

Wax, R.H. 1971. *Doing Fieldwork: Warnings and Advice*. Chicago: University of Chicago Press.

Weppner, R.S. 1977. *Street Ethnography*, Beverly Hills, Calif.: Sage.

Whyte, W.F. 1943, 1955, 1981. *Street Corner Society*. Chicago: University of Chicago Press. (Originally published in 1943: 2nd edn 1955: 3rd edn 1981.)

Wilkins, L.T. 1979. Human subjects – whose subject?, pp. 99–123 in C.B. Klockars and F.W. O'Connor (eds), *Deviance and Decency*. Beverly Hills, Calif.: Sage.

Wycoff, M.A. and Kelling, G.L. 1978 *The Dallas Experience: Organizational Reform*. Washington DC.: Police Foundation.

Yablonsky, L. 1968. *The Hippy Trip*. Harmondsworth: Penguin.

Zelditch, M. 1962. Some methodological problems of field studies, *American Journal of Sociology*, 67 (5): 556–576.

ABOUT THE AUTHOR

MAURICE PUNCH gained his BA at the University of Exeter and his MA and PhD in Sociology at the University of Essex. He was Lecturer in Sociology at Essex from 1970–75 and Visiting Lecturer at the State University of Utrecht from 1975–77. Since 1977 he has been Professor of Sociology at Nijenrode: The Netherlands School of Business. In 1981 he was Visiting Professor at the State University of New York at Albany, Rockefeller College, School of Criminal Justice. He has published widely on aspects of the police in English, Dutch and American journals and is author of the following books: *Progressive Retreat* (Cambridge, Cambridge University Press, 1977), *Policing the Inner City* (London: Macmillan; USA, distributed by Archon Books, Hampden, Conn.,1979), *Management and Control of Organizations* (Leiden/Antwerpen, Stenfert Kroese, 1981), *Control in the Police Organization* (ed.) (Cambridge, Mass., MIT Press, 1983), and *Conduct Unbecoming* (London, Tavistock Press, 1985). Professor Punch is chairperson at Nijenrode of the Department of Business and Society where he is currently working in the areas of deviant behavior, social responsibility, and control in business.

NOTES

NOTES

NOTES